C000055021

A True Sto

4 Sisters Battle Cancer

Tips to help with recovery and choices

By Amouraj Kellett

COPYRIGHT PAGE

The contents of this book represent my personal experiences which will differ to the experiences of other people involved.

I apologise to members of my family if any of the content causes distress.

I dedicate this book to

My Parents and siblings

Luke and Iris Kearns (My parents)

My sisters Bernadette, Anne, Pauline

My Brother Bernard

See pictures on my website amouraj.co.uk

CONTENT

Introduction

Introduction

The content of this book is raw. I have not worked with anyone else to write it or edit it. I had negotiated with an editor and was going to ask others to read it but changed my mind because should I be advised to change the wording or the story then it wouldn't reflect my thoughts and experiences. Yes there will be misuse of a comma or two but I am sure you will still get the gist of what my message is.   Being completely open about my experiences and feelings has been cathartic and I really hope you enjoy reading it.

I am just a normal woman who had a normal happy childhood, growing up on a council estate in Bradford. My father was an engineer/social worker and my mother was a school dinner lady. With four siblings, our home was a busy, loving and sometimes very competitive environment filled with happy memories. I explain more in chapter one. At the moment I live in a cute cottage in a beautiful part of North Yorkshire with my husband and adorable pooch named Whiskey. Our two children have their own busy lives and the most enormous gift and blessing is our gorgeous grandson. Working in medical sales, writing and general family life keeps me insanely busy as you can imagine.

Even though I unquestionably love all of the above, my life is not without stress, torment and days of feeling down, just like anyone else. The majority of the time my choices are to be extremely optimistic and positive. My friends would say laughter, fun and positivity are my personality traits. However, it is ok to not be happy and positive the whole time. This would make life exhausting don't you think? So do not ever question your abilities to cope with life or your strength to deal with challenges because you have a down day. Those days make us stronger and show us how to deal with challenging situations. In light of what I have just said, you will surely agree we all have our own shit to deal with. This is a true account of some of mine. Probably no worse or better than yours, just different. I unquestionably have a message or two to put out there. At worst my messages may not tempt your curiosity. At best, they will help you approach life with a new attitude or even assist in any similar choices you are faced with.

In 1988 my sister Bernadette passed away from breast cancer aged thirty-four. Two years later my father passed with pancreatic cancer and in 1995 my mother passed with throat cancer. Following this there was a break from trauma until 2011 when my two sisters and I were diagnosed with cancer within a month of each other. How fate deals its cards. We were all ill together and the only positive was that it enabled me to spend quality time with my sisters.

As I reflect on the various aspects of the past few years, my thoughts confirm how certain situations we have to deal with can make us stronger people. You may disagree and it has taken me such a long time to come to an understanding with myself that I am a different person to who I was then. I have diverse challenges. My physical appearance is different, not worse, maybe better but different. The after effects of the past six years have been testing on my strength as a human being. It was only after reaching my fifth year in remission did I feel like planning for the future.

Subconsciously those five years were like being on death row and now I am on parole for good behaviour. All of a sudden I became much more self-aware and recognised vital changes that needed to take place. I mean, I knew for sure my spirit had taken a massive hit, so for a long time my thoughts were dedicated to fixing myself.

My next series of books after this one are around "Mission Self Reset" which will explain how I executed fixing myself in detail – writing has empowered me to begin moving towards the best version of me. I knew I could not be a wife, a mother, a sister, a grandmother, a friend, a dog owner, a career woman until I could just be me. My capabilities of overcoming challenges were adding to my strengths as a person. Anything is possible. I had to keep moving forward thinking positive thoughts and to stop disliking the changes in my body because without those changes I wouldn't be me.

My outlook on life in general has changed confirming to me that our interactions and experiences make us who we are TODAY.

Why Amouraj Kellett?

During my treatment, at my lowest point when my hair, eyebrows, eyelashes were non-existent. My skin was dry and I generally felt like hiding under the duvet for like, ever. I would pick myself up, book myself a facial, go into town and treat myself to elegance with jewellery, body creams and scented candles. This would bring back the familiar feminine, elegant feelings that I could almost touch in the distance, knowing they were hanging around waiting for their time to return. Soon I began to realise how significant this was for my recovery, for confirming how considerably important my femininity was to me and for this reason I began to sell elegance to others. The name for this small business was Amouraj. Amour as you know is French for love – also AM = Anne

Marie, my sister who at the time was very ill herself and J for Jane. You have no idea how amazing it was to go to jewellery fayres and purchase beautiful pieces. I'd take buyers catalogues with me to see Anne when we would look, pick out pieces we liked and place the orders.

The following is an account of my journey which consists of Love, Loss and Survival. It is a journey with my sisters involving fun, laughter, blood, sweat and tears. The accounts of events are my personal views and opinions. Any persons involved in these events will have their own experiences that may differ from mine.

As you more than likely already know, genetics play a part in your wellbeing. The nature nurture theory believes our personality traits are made up of 50% our inherited genes and 50% our experiences. I ignored the lot and paid the price. Don't make the same mistake.

I seek to create awareness to the importance of listening to your body. It deserves to be desired, nurtured. It listens to you and acts upon your instructions. You are your own creation and your body will communicate with you without a doubt if it is struggling. So listen and act.

One of the first pioneers of creating self-awareness was the legendary Shirley Temple. She changed how other women felt and acted when diagnosed with cancer, encouraging them to speak out. In the autumn of 1972, Shirley noticed a lump in her left breast. In this decade cancer was a word that was whispered under your breath and if detected you lost all control of what happened next. Shirley Temple began the change in this behaviour and placed women on the road to having involvement in their treatment plan. She was one of the first celebrities to be vocal about her opinions on her diagnosis and treatment. This was extremely risky but after her surgery she insisted on holding a conference from her hospital bed. Against the surgeon's wishes, Shirley only had breast tissue removed instead of both her breasts and chest muscles. She wanted to inform other women of her decision. Horrifically at that time, quite often after the surgery, the initial diagnosis was proved to be incorrect. When this happened, the surgeons would tell you to be grateful you are cancer free and not to moan that you have had both breast removed, alongside your chest wall and all of your lymph nodes. Shirley demanded input into her treatment but it wasn't without aggravation. She was scolded for her audacity. She was a very brave woman.

CHAPTER ONE

Big Hair and shoulder Pads

Jeez I loved the 80s – I was in my early 20s and it was an amazingly special time to be young. The music was fab, the clothes were great. I used to make my own real leather miniskirts with negotiated deals on the go. Yeah I was a dealer! A hairdresser called Lucy would style my hair for free and in exchange I would supply her with tight leather mini skirts. For a period of time I worked as a secretary at an auctioneer company and one time, off cuts of leather in all kinds of colours were delivered to the warehouse. The banter with the guys in there was hilarious; we looked out for each other and they let me have the leather at a double double discount price of zero. My fingers were raw running up those man magnet minis. Word got around, business was booming and my pockets were, let's say, fruitful.

Looking back it was generally a worry free existence. At the time I felt challenged by some situations but in retrospect my life was pretty good. As I recall my feelings at the time, and I promise I can actually do that,

I had a loving family around me. I had an amazing boyfriend (now my husband) and wonderful friends. The thought of ever being without any members of my family were in a completely different world to reality. Those thoughts never entered my mind, if they had, I would have appreciated the special times we had together. One brother, three sisters and the most amazing parents, a perfect combination.

We were all very close as a family, especially growing up. Irish Catholics with a strict routine including church every Sunday without fail. I will say one word – Whitsuntide!!! What the hell was that all about? I don't know what it meant for the posh kids but for us, new socks, shoes, a coat and a straw hat! Very embarrassing. The memories of my youth are of an extremely fond nature. Nothing fancy, we lived on a council estate but it never bothered me once, right up to getting married. Our home was a lovely one, full of love and always someone visiting. Christmases were special. Not extravagant just special and all about family.

Pauline and I were a tag team; shiiit did we fight! But as we entered our teens we became much closer. I guess we took after our father, Luke Kearns, who founded the Irish society in our town. He was expelled from Priest College in Ireland – legend! He came over to England in the potato famine, met mum at a dance. Mums parents were very wealthy and not impressed with dad at all. They tried tirelessly to discourage their relationship and never even attended their wedding. Five kids later with major ups and downs, they stayed married to the end. Mum was a dinner lady at my school growing up and Dad was a hard worker who provided for his family. He also was a Labour Councillor, and founder of the local community office where he ran a tight ship made up of community workers helping people on the estate.

He was a really good man and I have memories of women banging on our door in the middle of the night after being physically abused and dad spending the next few hours finding them a place to stay before going to work at 6am. One year a family on the estate had experienced major hardship, the father being sent to prison. It was Christmas Eve. We wrapped up toys and took them to the family alongside food for them to have a lovely Christmas dinner the next day. Let us bear in mind; my parents had five children and only one wage.

I had a really close bond with my father which grew rapidly at the age of two when I was seriously injured in a road accident. The first of my nine lives. Hospital was my home for numerous weeks as my injuries were a fractured skull, two broken legs and a broken pelvis. I have vivid memories of being in hospital and my rehabilitation. One of those distinct memories is being sitting in my hospital bed with my legs in pullies and my parents at the ward entrance waving goodbye. Growing up my dad took me everywhere with him. One fond memory was being five years old at the wool exchange Christmas fayre in Bradford and it was snowing so heavy. Dad was Santa and I was his fairy. Mum had made me such a fairytale costume with wings. We walked across the balcony and down the stairs; the hall was packed to the door, such a treasured memory.

As I grew and became a teenager, obviously my Dad became embarrassing as Dads do and our bond lessened. It happens. However I always have and always will have a special love for him. I really wish I could hug them both and let them know how incredibly special they were.

Some years ago my dad wrote a book about his life which was made into a play. At the time Pauline and I were very busy being annoyingly young and I am ashamed to say, for some reason we never read it. Life got in the way and over the years it was passed around and misplaced. We recently asked around and my nephew found a copy on an old email address. I began reading, not sure what I was expecting but I could not put it down. It was nothing short of amazing. I feel so close to my father right now! Regretting not reading it when he was alive, learning and understanding the difficulties he faced in his youth but also how he loved and protected his family. I am enormously proud of him.

At Christmas Pauline and I generally received the same gifts but would be playing with them weeks before. Bernadette bought us both a massive selection box but by the time she came to wrap them they were empty. She was fuming. I was only about three when Pauline would find the presents and insisted play with them.

One year she opened her typewriter Christmas morning and there was a letter in it saying "my name is Pauline Kearns" - we were like the terrible twins!

We were very close as teenagers working at bars in Bradford Centre and partied together which pleased mum as she could relax and sleep when we were out until early hours of the morning. We would roll in, freezing, wearing next to nothing and mum would have our beds warm for us with electric blankets.

I was the wild one and would force my sister into situations that would make her feel uncomfortable. Money was minimal so there was no way I would ever pay for a taxi home. I am sure you can all relate to this but part of the evening was dedicated to finding a lift. It was usually two policemen who would be patrolling outside the club. They would wait and give us a lift home, telling the sergeant on his "walkie talkie" or whatever it was then. "We have just rescued two girls and they need escorting to safety. Of course there was no funny business being such a prude but we gave them a sneaky snog when we got home. This one time when we came out of the club they were nowhere to be found. However a couple of guys who we had been talking to offered us a ride home. Pauline said "no way Jane" "come on Pauline, yes way! I'm skint" - next thing we knew we were rocketing up the wrong side of Manchester road at 110mph. The driver had turned mental ffs!!! Pauline was crying in the front while I was snogging and laughing in the back but then realised how bad the situation was and demanded he let us out. By this time we were in peel park where someone had been murdered two days before - Pauline jumped out crying – running after her I was on a mission, it was three in the morning and freezing!!. But no way was she getting back in that car. Shit, she was so sensible and it irritated the life out of me. We were rushing through the park in complete darkness like little startled rabbits, searching for the exit. They guys caught up with us. Thankfully they came to their senses and drove us home safely (THEY didn't get a snog). Some of the stuff we did was hilarious!! In fact all my sisters, brother and my parents had the most incredible sense of humor.

In the 80s, on the few evenings I would stay in, we would all sit around the TV knitting and watching Dallas. I know! Lame yeah! A normal loving family with no dramas as far as my world was aware of. All the family gathered around the table for Sunday Lunch. There were always family get togethers, especially at Christmas. A complete jigsaw – I never imagined it would be any different forever and eternity.

What do I remember about the 80s – going to live aid and crying with all the females when Brian sang Slave to Love, going to USA twice on a limited budget and discovering when I got there, my uncle was an uber rich millionaire so we lived it large on his yacht, flew in his helicopter down Miami Beach. I can taste the cocktails and hear the music. I had no knowledge of growing old; it just wouldn't happen to me. My 80s favorites were Mark King from Level 42, I just loved him. 5 star, Pretty in Pink, back to the future. Then came the thong generation. What was that all about? No wonder they were so angry, it was like walking around with a permanent wedgie.

CHAPTER TWO

The c word - shhh!

One part of the 80s I didn't enjoy was my introduction to the C word, Cancer. That's what it was like then, it was whispered mid-sentence so no one could hear. Growing up all of my father's sisters had passed with either breast or ovarian cancer so inevitably there was a lot of whispering going on.

I was twenty four and my sister Bernadette was thirty two when she had a cyst removed from her breast. She showed me the wounds. I was mortified having never seen anything like it. It was extremely terrifying as this was the first hint of there being a shift in what was perceived to be a traumatic free family. Bernadette was divorced with two young children so relied heavily on my parents for emotional support.

Two years later she found another lump and assumed it was another cyst. Visiting the GP, she worryingly told him saying "it doesn't feel like the previous cyst" The Doctor sent her for a biopsy and was told she would hear in due course regarding the results. She waited and waited and waited. No news is good news right? They lost her details and never sent for her. Six months later the lump was the size of a grapefruit. She had lost all feeling in her arm. So mum said she needed to ring up the hospital, which Bernadette did but they couldn't find her details – she wasn't on the list. She was given an appointment and was entered on the system once again.

After being diagnosed with Breast Cancer she had the lump removed.

Bernadette was given no chemo but radiotherapy instead. I remember the traumatic state she was in as whilst having the radiotherapy so close to the operation, it re opened her wounds. Dad wanted to investigate the reasons why her details were lost and take legal action against the hospital but Bernadette feared it would have an impact on the way she was treated so he respected her wishes.

Her boyfriend at the time finished their relationship because he found the whole situation too traumatic which left Bernadette emotionally distraught. My poor sister got back on her feet and went back to work as a supervisor at the local hospital restaurant. As anyone who has been associated with Breast Cancer knows, after treatment a drug called Tamoxifen would be prescribed to mimic estrogen (the estrogen feeds breast cancer cells). The drug would throw you into menopause which came with exacerbated side effects. Bernadette hated the side effects (hot flushes, sick, bone pain) so her GP advised her to stop taking the medication which she did. A couple of months later at an appointment with her consultant she informed him of the decision. He completely hit the roof screaming "why have you done that?" Bernadette said she would start taking it again but he warned it could be too late. I am not sure if she took it or not after that. Stopping the medication was disastrous. Losing her notes, advising to stop her medication – and to think we rely on these people to save our lives!

A few months later after having a massive fit, Bernadette was rushed into hospital. Fluid was drained from her lungs and sadly she was diagnosed with lung cancer. It was a very sad, confusing, traumatic time for the family as she was so young, only 33. Scans took place. The consultant had the dreaded conversation with Dad. She had full body, terminal cancer. He proceeded to advise my devastated father "we can get her back on her feet so she can go home but you have to tell her the truth. It is vital she has the opportunity immediately to sort things for her children" Dad came home to tell us and made everyone promise not to breathe a word to her.

Paul, her boyfriend came back on the scene and they grew very close. He wanted to get married but she wouldn't because she felt it was for the wrong reasons. Immediately she had minimal chemo however the cancer quickly accelerated to her spine, bones and brain.

She was in and out of hospital. We visited her once to find her in a state on the floor. She'd had a fit and there was no bed guard. Another time we came into her room and she had just been told it was in her brain. I will never forget that moment; we all froze – Mum, Dad, Me, Anne, Pauline. Bernadette just sat on the bed crying. I walked over, put my arms around her and told her we loved her – she sobbed. Everyone came and hugged her. It was a situation where no one knew what to say or do but the only thing we could do was love her.

Bernadette always seemed to have some kind of sixth sense. We all used to meet at Mums on Saturday mornings and periodically she would enlighten the group of sisters that she'd had one of her weird dreams. We really looked forward to catching up; coffee and gossip was how it went. I remember one time she had dreamt the night before that she woke up suddenly to hear banging on the door. She ran down the stairs in her pajamas thinking there must have been a plane crash because there was fire everywhere outside but the thing she couldn't understand was that everyone in the chaos were wearing Bradford City football shirts. How eerie!! Probably just a coincidence but about 18 months later the tragic fire enveloped the Bradford City Ground. Like I said it was probably a coincidence. However, I remember before she got ill she swapped me her old wedding rings. I cannot remember what for, probably some boots or a bag. I was only about 19 and secretly pawned them to pay for a holiday in Italy. When she was really ill in hospital, I visited her from work but she was fast asleep so I just sat beside her reading the paper. All of a sudden she said to me "Jane, why did you pawn my rings" I gasped and shot to my feet to see she was still fast asleep. That really freaked me out because I told no one about that.

Poor Bernadette deteriorated very quickly. She had to move into my parents' house with the children so she could be looked after properly. Her bed was in the living room. Every evening we all would kneel around and say the rosary – It was all my parents could turn to as they watched helplessly their second child be taken from them.

Personally for me the rosary thing was terrifying. It was dark and the whole situation was distressing but my parents were devout Catholics and believed by praying to god it would help in some way. Desperate times call for desperate measures. As human beings, when we find ourselves in despairing situations where death is inevitable and there is nothing left to do, all you have left is faith and prayer.

One time I was alone with her, sat on her bed doing her nails. She looked me in the eye and said "Jane, you and I have been through a lot together. I have been the best sister I could be to you. Tell me please the truth! AM I DYING?" You have no idea how I felt at that moment – she was staring into my eyes, looking for my reaction and expression. I considered telling her the truth but I respected my fathers' wishes and told her I didn't know as I hadn't asked anyone that question. We both cried.

We all took turns to stay up with her all night as she couldn't be left alone. One time it was my shift and Anne stayed with me. We all chatted about lots of things including babies and boyfriends. Due to the drugs and also her condition, Bernadette would constantly see people sat on her bed and talk to them. She thought she had something stuck to her finger and kept shaking it off. Well, Anne and I were trying our best not to laugh but we couldn't help it. "Are you two laughing at me?" We all burst out laughing!!

Another time I stayed the night with her alone and brought her chocolates. I was shattered and fell asleep in the chair which was bad I know. I felt her shaking me in my sleep. I woke up "sorry Jane did I wake you?" she really didn't want to be alone. "I have saved you a chocolate" she had eaten the lot and saved me one - bless her!

I called in to see her one day after work and she was in bed trawling through the mail order catalogue. "What are you doing?" I asked. "Jane sit down here beside me and let me hold your hand" so I did "Dad has told me today that I have only days left to live so I am buying Christmas presents for the children". She was so calm like she had a weight lifted from her shoulders. We sat and cuddled, talked and cuddled. Then a week later I received the dreaded phone call.

CHAPTER THREE

"The Greatest Love of All"

It was October18th 1988, 6am, still dark, drizzling and very foggy. The phone rang, it was Mum "you better come across Jane, Bernadette is asking for you". Oh my god, I knew exactly what mum was saying. My heart sank to my toes. I quickly dressed and jumped in the car. The journey down was one I will never forget. It was a feeling of sheer anxiety and fear of what I was going to face but most of all sadness, complete sadness. When I entered my parents' house all I remember was the sense of a sad cloud throughout. Rushing to her bedside, Bernadette was sat on the edge of the bed with Mum at her side holding her hand. I know dad had been up with her through the night and she had deteriorated rapidly. She was trying to say things but it was just noise, she couldn't actually say words – then she said Jane as clear as anything. Mum had been trying all morning to get her to lie in bed "you will be more comfortable" Mum whispered but Bernie was having none of it.

For days Bernadette had been in and out of reality. One minute she would be talking as normal as you or I and the next she would be in a completely different place which was a combination of the drugs and the deterioration of the brain tumor. I visited the night before when Bernie had been having a conversation with Mum. "Mum, I am so frightened, where am I going to go? What is going to happen to me?" Mum tried her hardest to comfort her. She talked to her about heaven and how wonderful it would be. "But who will come for me and take me there, I always thought it would be you or Dad but no one will come for me" "don't worry" Mum replied "angels will come for you" "Mum don't leave me in church overnight please as I will be frightened on my own, Let me stay here until the funeral" Mum promised to look after her.

Anne and Pauline came and we laid her gently into bed. She was in pain and the doctor didn't know what to do. To be honest it seemed quite chaotic. He said she was dying. Bernadette was constantly groaning but the last word she said as clear as anything was "angels" and that is the truth! It was a surreal experience like I was out of body just watching the situation take place. To my right Anne was telling her she loved her and to watch over her and to my left was Pauline, who looked in a complete state of shock. Then suddenly the three of us came together and started to sing her favorite song by Whitney Houston – The greatest love of all. This seemed to calm her down. I noticed a lonely tear slowly roll down her cheek so she could hear that we were all there for her in her last moment. I am so sorry Bernadette you had to leave this world before you were ready, when you had so much you wanted to do with your life. That day I lost the first piece of my heart which would never been replaced.

Sat here writing this now, it is hard to believe we have been so long without her. She never experienced mobile phones or the internet – how weird is that. She has missed out on the joys of being a grandma. I know if she was here, it would be her instigating sister holidays, Christmas parties and we would spend hours on the phone. It would be certain she would be obsessed with Facebook, displaying her love for her children and grandchildren. That is just the person she was.

Following the funeral I wanted to channel my sadness into something positive so I organised a fancy dress football match with my work colleagues and customers who were local pharmacists. We raised around £5,000. This was used to buy a machine at Bradford War on Cancer which would separate blood cells. The machine had a gold plaque on it inscribed "Bernadette Thompson 1954 – 1988"

Are you aware that chemotherapy was developed at Bradford University in the 1950/60s ⍰

George Watson and Robert Turner were deeply moved by the young mothers suffering from breast cancer, many of whom would not live to see their children grow up. "I found wards full of women basically awaiting death in the majority of cases," said Professor Turner in a later interview "In those days there was no treatment beyond surgery and radiotherapy." They had become dissatisfied with conventional approaches to cancer treatment – they believed that more effective treatment could be accomplished by looking at breast cancer as a systemic disease right from the start and started to look for a further advance that could treat (and possibly prevent) the widespread dissemination of cancer throughout the body.

Robert Turner himself worked alongside Professor John Wilkinson in Manchester during the early 50s furthering this work and when he came to work in Bradford he decided that this could be put to good use in breast cancer too.

In combination with surgery, they tried their new treatment on 34 women aged between 23 and 74 suffering from various stages of cancer, many of whom had gone beyond the capabilities of conventional treatment. These patients were told the exact truth about their conditions, they had an advanced disease, it was thought this new treatment could help and would they like to try it?

The results were dramatic – they soon found that giving them both together actually enhanced their individual effects. Thirty of the thirty-four patients showed marked inhibition5. While there were complications, as there would be with any treatment, some patients were cured in just two months - including a case of breast cancer during pregnancy, which was usually extremely serious. Most encouragingly, there was also a high level of response from cancers that had spread to bone and soft tissues.

Staggered by the effectiveness of the treatment, Watson and Turner immediately switched the frontline treatment for breast cancer at the Bradford Royal Infirmary from surgery combined with radiotherapy to surgery combined with chemotherapy and set about publishing their results in the British Medical Journal

(Toil, tears and triumph-the story of the pioneering of chemotherapy in Bradford / War on Cancer News, issue 3, spring 1997)

My parents, as you would imagine took the loss of Bernadette extremely hard which was tough given they now had to raise her two children. They were both strong Catholics but faith wasn't enough, they just couldn't cope. It broke their hearts and two years later we were sat in the same room with my lovely father when he passed away due to pancreatic cancer aged 68. Five years after that it was Mum. Throat Cancer took her aged 70. It was a harsh few years for us all. Looking back it left me feeling very vulnerable. For the first time in my life I felt alone. No unconditional parental love. Now writing about it I can see answers to some of the feelings I experienced. All of a sudden I had two babies to which I gave all my love but who would give it to me, my husband? Yes of course but what if he let me down. I began inwardly to need love and acceptance and didn't know how to deal with this. I couldn't rationalize it within myself so I certainly couldn't talk to anyone about it. It is then I started along the path of learning to love myself, to trust only myself and to be my own best friend and confident. This really makes a lot of sense to me now.

I was by this time in my thirty fifth year, the children were small and my husband was building a successful career in the motor trade. He was dealer principle for Mercedes in Manchester. Later he progressed to managing Ferrari, Maserati and Porsche. His career progression was accompanied with many life enhancing experiences which we look back on with exhilarating memories such as dancing at Naomi Campbell's birthday party. Crazy I know but true. I reflect on some of these memories in one of the chapters. Appreciation is a wonderful concept isn't? Like most things you get caught up in life and believe good times are forever. Aging? What the hell was that? It wasn't going to happen to me for sure.

CHAPTER FOUR

The in-between years

Throughout my 20's I set up and facilitated two support groups. Both groups brought together sufferers of Anorexia/Bulimia (The subject of a future book). This, and finding myself in the unfortunate circumstances surrounding the recent bereavements in my family, conveys my motives at this particular time to educate myself. Primarily securing a certificate in counselling (City and Guilds), which then led to a three year, full time degree stint at university to study psychology. This was accompanied by its own challenges such as raising two small children and working part time. My degree led me to work with a couple of projects at a hospital (clinical psychology department) in a neighboring town promoting healthy living in the community, writing and presenting a course on "listening Skills" and once again coordinating a support group for Anorexia and Depression.

I was offered a permanent position at the hospital and funding to study for my masters in Clinical Psychology. At this particular time my husband had taken promotion in his career which led to the family moving to York, a neighboring city. The difficult decision was made to take a break from psychology altogether and that judgment led me to the career I am in today (Medical Sales). It was a tough decision but the right one for me. Little did

I know the pleasure this career would give me over the years. Being very good at what I do, my success is a testament to how hard I work. It really does tick so many boxes – the boxes I compiled whilst sat in an office many moons ago, trapped between four walls and feeling extremely unfulfilled. It feels so liberating jumping out of bed in the morning knowing it is going to be so much different to yesterday. Every day brings new challenges and experiences. I get to drive around beautiful North Yorkshire, meeting interesting customers to educate them on a lifesaving drug. My career has taken me around the world to such places as Dubai, Italy, Egypt, Croatia, USA and many more. What is not to like? It is hard work but they pay me a good salary, therefore they deserve my best efforts.

There have been two occasions when I have been bursting with contentment in my current career. Each company I have worked for I have always formed lasting relationships with colleagues. One company we had a circle of trust and would always stick together on company conferences. The conferences were amazing. I can only compare them to going on incredible holidays with friends. Then there was the dream team. There were no set rules. Just bring in the business they said and that is what we did. We were number one in the country.

Coming up to 2011 – we lived in quite a large family home with two demanding teenagers who brought lots of excitement, unpredictability, trauma, challenges but I wouldn't have had it any other way. The home was constantly busy. My mother in law (Dolly) was in her 80s and spent so much time with us. I really loved her and we got along like mother and daughter. One day she came to stay and never went home.

CHAPTER FIVE
AmouraJ (Anne Marie)

It was summer 2011. I remember the day, even the actual minute so well - I had just come out of a nurse meeting in Selby. The sun was blaring down. The day before, I had bought new sunglasses so I pulled over to find them. As I searched impatiently, the phone rang - it was my sister Anne. "Hiya" I said happily. "Jane" she replied "I have something to tell you" immediately, I sat upright. I knew whatever it was, this needed my full attention. She proceeded to tell me that she had been diagnosed with Kidney cancer. This floored me completely; I was not expecting it at all. What do you say to something like that? The conversation continued with reassurance of my love for her and my commitment to be there for her night and day no matter what. "Please help me Jane, I am scared"

"Of course I will help you. Don't be scared, you will get through this Anne and I will be by your side the whole time, I am coming over" I remember clearly telling her that she was the strong one and if anyone could beat this it would be her. When I arrived she was sat on the patio with her husband and my other sister Pauline. We chatted about the diagnosis. I knew she had not been feeling well. We sat together a couple of weeks earlier at her sons' wedding (he married in Spain but had a second celebration in Bradford). Anne told me she was worried about the way she felt. She told me that at the wedding in Spain, after two glasses of wine she felt so drunk, like never before and it was worrying her. I never expected it to be so serious.

Anne was such a character. She was beautiful, loving and a mother figure to me. She was so thoughtful, caring and so much fun to be with. Any problems she was there and had all the answers. Anne had a sense of humor second to none. However, we knew not to cross her - boy was she feisty!! New Year's Eve a good few years ago, her teenage boys went into town to celebrate in their new Christmas designer clothes. The bars were so busy they were separated and the middle one was attacked and made to hand over the expensive gear he was wearing and had just been given for Christmas. He had to walk home freezing in his underwear. Anne was like a vigilante gone mad. She hunted them down like a wolf, fully armed and dangerous with a...... MOP. Yes a mop, what the hell would she have done if she found them? Clean them to death? We laughed massively and I loved being her sister.

So as I told you, we were sat on the patio drinking tea, discussing the diagnosis. For a while Anne had backache but put it down to the fact she was sat in a draft at work. This is the honest truth – the only reason she went to the doctors was because her and her husband kept hearing music playing in the house and couldn't find where it was coming from. Then it turned into banging, like someone was dropping a pile of heavy books. Even Pauline heard it. Anne said she felt someone was trying to tell her something so she made an appointment at the doctors. The doctor felt her stomach and sent her straight to the hospital as her kidney was so swollen. She had a scan and the next day was told it was cancer and very serious, Stage 4. Anne could not believe what she was hearing, this was devastating news as you can imagine.

After the death of Bernadette, Mum and Dad - Anne, Pauline, Bernard and I were quite close. Although we had our own busy lives, we were always there for each other and Anne was like the mother figure, always sorting out our problems etc. A few years ago Anne and I had a massive fall out over a complete misunderstanding but it escalated and we ended up not speaking for quite a while.

Anne was really busy with her boys who played in a band "White light Parade". They played in London quite a lot. They had been so close to a signing so many times. One of their songs was featured in a Tom Cruise movie. Anne was incredibly proud of them. I attended a couple of the gigs with her, witnessing the pride and immense pleasure they felt as parents of three handsome, talented boys.

Being busy myself with work and my own family, we evidently drifted apart. Then a couple of years later I received a lovely Christmas card from Anne with a letter inside which I carry with me always. It means so much to me and I feel so lucky to have it.

"Dear Jane,

A couple of months ago I got some meat lodged in my throat, it was really bad and I thought I was going to die (sounds dramatic but it was really bad). My life flashed before me and I thought about you, I had deep regret that we have not kept in touch more and I did not want to die without letting you know how much I love you and how much you mean to me. So I want to let you know this Christmas that I love you Jane xxxxx"

Love Anne

I really cried.

After that Day sat on the Patio, Anne and I kept in touch every day and I visited her two or three times a week. It doesn't sound much and I wish it could have been more frequent but Anne lived in Bradford and I lived in York. Working full time didn't help the situation either but it was what it was. Soon this would change and we would see each other so much more.

The cancer had spread rapidly. Anne was scheduled for an operation to remove her kidney. However after one of her scans they decided not to operate as the cancer was too advanced. Her family proceeded to fight against this and went straight to the top at the NHS. Eventually they relented and operated giving her eight months to live. Following the operation Anne soon was on her feet and thankfully the operation gave her an extra two years.

Seriously, I have had a mental block and not written anything for a month. Now facing up to the full picture, which I knew all along, writing and recalling the situation with Anne is very painful. Not that any previous situations with my other sister or parents were not agonizing. I just realize that I could detach myself somewhat from the events surrounding them. However, with Anne, I couldn't. The reason being, I lived it with her. I felt her fear and on top of that I was living with my own difficulty. I would disconnect myself from reality like it was lingering on the outside of my body. I could touch it however it was not allowed to enter my spirit. Having said that it fought its way in, long after my treatment ended, breaking my spirit for a short period of time. Anyway this is the reason I couldn't detach myself from the painful feelings associated with Anne because I was too busy detaching myself from my own.

CHAPTER SIX

The day my life changed forever

Anne was diagnosed in July 2011 and it was now early September which is a time of the year I love. Still warm, the leaves starting to turn a beautiful shade of brown. Things were changing at work. I felt extremely lucky. Although the team I was in was folding, the prospects for my career were looking great. I loved working North Yorkshire with a passion. At the time I was promoting a device for COPD. Even though I was happy, the summer had not been without its anxieties.

My manager at the time was a great guy, ex forces from Sandhurst. He sat me down and told me he had put me forward for a promotion. There were two others going for it but he said it had my name on it and he had told the people interviewing that I was perfect for the job. I had the most experience and achievements. Really, it was just a formality.

I did all the prep and had my brag file bursting at the seams but didn't get the job - I couldn't understand why but looking back I found it difficult to drum up any enthusiasm. I just wanted to get out, get home and go to bed.

The following three days I spent on the sofa. Not sick - just immensely tired. I have never felt anything like it. Like someone had put a straw in my ear and sucked the life out of me. Not being a frequent visitor at the doctors, reluctantly I made an appointment. He sent me for some blood tests but the form stayed pinned to my notice board and I never went. Also I never attended my appointment for a mammogram. They sent me another appointment which I also nearly missed because I was just too tired and couldn't be bothered (Mammograms have been an annual event since the death of Bernadette) Thank god I decided to go.

Returning to work after having the tired spell on the sofa was a struggle. It wasn't just tired; it was so tired I literally could not lift my head up. Anyway it was a lovely day as the September days seem to be, clear sky and very warm. I remember being sat in the study doing my emails before heading out to meetings. My plans were to visit Anne as usual after work. Hearing an almighty screech of breaks outside the window, I shot to my feet to see a small child screaming. Dashing outside to investigate, to my horror a black cat had been hit by a car right outside the window and killed. Immediately my thoughts were drawn to the superstitious circumstances and feared my day was about to get worse.

On my return from visiting Anne I noticed my unopened mail from the morning. Quickly ploughing my way through it I came to a letter from the hospital inviting me back following my mammogram. It didn't register really but immediately my thoughts were I should just go and not tell anyone knowing how much David worries about stuff. However, my apprehension got the better of me deciding to tell him and Dolly (his Mum who was living with us at the time). Playing it down, I could see the worry in his face.

We rocked up for my appointment the next day. I was not anxious or worried as of course it was going to be a mistake. While having a scan, the consultant told me she was very concerned about what she could see and needed to do a biopsy immediately. It was now becoming a little more disturbing. Anyone who has had one will know how uncomfortable and painful a procedure this is. Basically they kind of shoot a needle into your breast which grabs tissue and pulls it out. The suggestion was to bring David into the room for the results. Much to my disbelief the words were carefully chosen - a presence of hormonal breast cancer. "oh right what now" - well, my mind automatically hit the auto reject button - that information is not wanted so it is null and void - the life drained from David's face. Sally, the breast nurse who was assigned to me to organise my care pathway, explained the scan had shown quite a large lump in my left breast and I would need the full works to give me the best chance of survival. David and I just looked at each other "fuck me!!!" Sally told me the ins and outs of what was going to happen, it went in one ear and out the other. Nothing could have prepared me for the reality of the situation. I didn't complain, just wanted to get on with it and carry on as normal. "You will put about two stone on" she whispered "WHAT!" Now I was fooking panicking!!! This proves, I was not accepting how serious this was. My thoughts were, kick me while I'm down why don't you. Not only am I going to be bald but I'm going look like fucking paddy from

Emmerdale (I love paddy BTW) luckily I didn't put too much weight on. I have the dog walking to thank for that. I did gain a few pounds I'm not going to lie but that was the least of my worries.

Being the strong one and the carer - my role kicked in immediately alongside my determination not to let it take over my life.   Sally asked me in her soft voice if I had any thoughts on what I would like to happen in terms of surgery. I was very clear that I wanted both breasts taken off and implants put in. Every cloud and all that!! She replied with admiration for my decisiveness and booked me in with the best surgeon for this procedure.

We left the hospital and returned to the car without saying a word. Poor David, he looked terrified. My thoughts were, this must be the moment I am supposed to burst into tears but

1. I really didn't want to cry.

2. I had to be strong for my family.

We decided to tell the kids as they were 19 and 16, as you can imagine they were very upset. My daughter was particularly concerning as ever since she was about three she had this fear of me dying and leaving her for some reason. Georgia was seeing Charlie at the time and Chris had just started seeing Nikki - so they both had someone close to talk to apart from me and Dad. Dolly (David's mum) was amazing - My love for her was immense, she was like a second mum to me. I would just like to say she was a valuable part of my recovery and for that my promise to her was to always look after her, which I did and will talk about that later.

Certainty is a humanistic need. We all need a degree of certainty in our lives to function as human beings. Personally I thrive on stability. However through my own experiences, I have quickly learned to accept and deal with uncertainty when it arises. I was absolutely in a situation where my future was uncertain. My thermostat for uncertainty changed very quickly and suddenly the little things didn't seem to matter anymore. This uncertainty was raw and physical.

My employers were fantastic and the sales director called me and said she would take the worry of money away. They paid me full pay throughout my absence with the use of my company car. This may sound dull but I just didn't talk about it much after that. David came home with books and links to sites for me to research but I never read or searched one thing. Nothing could be changed and I was living it so why would I want to read about it. It would be more imploring to loose myself in a book, taking me to another world far away from this one.

Visiting Anne became my priority - she couldn't believe this was happening to us. I would drive over to Bradford to visit her. Anne, Pauline and I became closer than ever. It was this time when Anne was having problems in terms of her surgery and them refusing to operate. Her sons fought for her rights to have the operation to remove her kidney and eventually they gave in.

Having private healthcare, my first appointment with my surgeon was at the Nuffield in York. Mr Munot was a really caring, endearing doctor and we immediately struck up a very trusting relationship. My consultation was extremely difficult for both David and myself. This may sound crude but we were quite physical and my breasts were an enormous part of my femininity. I have always tried to take pride in my appearance and my full breasts complimented my curves. I'm sorry if that sounds a weird thing to say but that was how I was feeling in my consultation. It was surreal - I was sat on the consultation table naked from the waist up, David sat at the other side of the curtain listening to us discussing removing my greatest assets but what was the alternative. This was going to save my life - bring it on!!!!!!

He booked me in for the 22nd December, Christmas week.

CHAPTER SEVEN

A Chill in the Atmosphere

22nd December 2011

It was 5am on the day of my surgery. Bag packed and my tummy empty. Not nervous at all, in fact I've been more anxious before a dental appointment. I was in control - Georgia's school things sorted - routine mapped out for the dog (whiskey) - David and I set off for the Nuffield, we had to be there for 7am. The journey down is engraved in my memory forever, still dark with morning mist. How could I be so calm- it's like the reason for this trip had been erased from my mind. However, there was definitely a chill in the atmosphere. Dave held my hand the whole way. He is often baffled at how I deal with certain situations, it's just how I am, unconsciously programming my psyche to manage difficulties and it works for me.

We arrived at 6.40 and were shown to my private room where I changed into the hospital gown. First the anesthetists came to talk about pain relief etc. He was not as warm as I might expect, a bit aloof but not to worry. He was followed by my lovely Mr Munot who proceeded to do his markings for the surgery. The nurse informed me I was due to go down in ten minutes. She advised Dave he may as well go home, he replied he would come back in the afternoon as we were informed I should be back in my room by then. When he left, my fluffy slippers paced the room until the nurse came for me. We walked down to the theatre chatting - she was trying to distract my thoughts. As we approached the theatre I was shaking - fuck! I'm not in control. The nurses were lovely - in the prep room it is always calm and in previous ops, the seconds before you drop off into your deep sleep has been an amazing feeling but this was different, much different. There was no presence of that lovely fuzzy feeling it was just out zzzzzzzzz.

The next bit shocked me to my core!!!

The surgery being performed was basically a double mastectomy with expandables, which meant they would be injected monthly, expanding them to the size required. At a later date the expandables would be replaced with implants. It was a lengthy op, about 5 hours normally. It was a new way of doing the procedure in terms of utilising what was possible of the skin already surrounding the breast to make them more natural. The downside was that the possibility of rejection and infection was high, in which case he would have to revert back to the old way of using back muscle. Mr Munot stated later that mine were the best outcome he had had so far - get in!!!!!

Anyway back to 22nd December 2011 - David, Dolly and the kids came back in the afternoon as promised with gifts and love. The nurse advised them to go back home as there had been complications and they wouldn't see me awake any time soon. My loved ones still wanted to see me - aw bless!! They were quite shocked when led into the private room. Georgia recalls being told I was on life support. To her it must have looked that way with tubes all over me. It just shows how scared she was. They walked to the lift in silence; Dolly broke down and cried while David and the kids remained silent.

Half way through the surgery I had respiratory depression. In other words I had been given too much morphine or had a reaction to it causing me to stop breathing. Immediately a morphine reversal was given and the priority was to regain my breathing and finish the surgery unfortunately without any pain relief. I woke up during the surgery however, fortunately I cannot remember thank god - extra anesthetic was given which is why I didn't surface until the evening. Opening my eyes, the pain hit me like a train and panic took over. My bed was surrounded with nurses and doctors including Mr Munot, all waiting for me to wake, it was chaotic. He started to explain that I was not allowed pain relief until I woke but would now be given a paracetamol IV as they couldn't risk anything stronger. He asked me if I could remember anything about the op. I could not remember but couldn't answer as I was continuously vomiting which was difficult with an oxygen mask. The pain was unbearable and I was pleading with them to make it stop. Everyone was trying to make me as comfortable as possible and eventually I drifted back off to sleep. My family came back but I cannot remember seeing them.

Being in a private room was ultimate comfort; the nurses couldn't do enough for me. It was really cozy, snuggly warm with TLC on tap. The next day things started to settle down. The pain was bearable and the results were looking good - I was pretty chuffed actually. I always loved my breasts and there was an intense sadness at losing them as they had served me so well. Nevertheless the thought of having pert, firm ones appealed enormously. I felt very lucky to have a positive outcome with two symmetrical double Ds.

Christmas Eve came, still in my comfy hospital bed having really cozy sleeps. The visitors today were continuous - my family and friends were amazingly supportive. It wasn't until the evening when darkness set in and silence was surrounding me that it felt surreal to be alone in my bed. Being the only patient in the hospital I had two choices - sit here and feel sorry for myself or make this a memorable Christmas Eve - ffs drains in each hand like two little handbags (draining fluid from my op), my chocolates under one arm, I began to shuffle my way to the nurses station. Laura Croft had nothing on me. "I'm here to spoil your fun" I smiled approaching them and from that moment on we never stopped laughing until the early hours. We raided the fridge, we sang, danced (as much as you can with two drains exiting your body). I was exhausted. So much so the nurses literally had to carry me back to my bed and I slept like a baby.

I woke Christmas morning very excited to be going home. The nurses had been ace but the thought of spending the day with my family was the best Christmas present ever. The kids refused to open any gifts without me. Before leaving the hospital my drains had to be removed. The nurse sheepishly whispered I'm not going to lie this is not pleasant. It was not nice let's just say that but I was free and could go home. David picked me up and I had a wonderful Christmas at home being looked after, cared for and loved.

My recovery was remarkable. Being totally happy with my surgery results, I just could not stop looking at them in the mirror. Optimism had set in and I knew I could cope with anything.

Never once did I think I may die. As usual living in the moment had been my savior. It took a while to get on my feet but my speedy recovery was down to many factors, my positive attitude, alongside the support from my family and friends. My wonderful dog whiskey never left my side from the moment I arrived home and walking him throughout this process was a support mechanism which seemed critical to keeping me sane. The exercise helped my energy levels. My family fussed around me and I had jumped the first hurdle towards the finishing line.

Due to being at home recovering, Dolly and I spent every day together and became very close. We talked for hours about her younger years. It really fascinated me that she was a teenager during the war. Frequenting the dances and dating the American soldiers. She always said I was the daughter she never had. People would comment - how could I have my mother in law living with me but I loved having her with us. I cared so much about her. She was in her 80s but looked and acted much younger.

January 2012

My recovery was quick having great healing skin. Thank god I didn't know what was coming. I couldn't have got through my chemotherapy without my Dolly and for that I promised her I would look after her.

Returning for my follow up appointment, Mr Munot informed me that there were traces of cancer in my lymph nodes so I would have to have them removed in January before starting my chemo in February. The procedure took place to remove some of my lymph nodes in my left arm. It was a straight forward op with no complications. There have been no problems with the drainage in my arm thank god. When having lymph nodes removed it is common for the arm to swell and be extremely painful - luck is on my side so far. If you have had your lymph nodes removed you should be careful not to put your arm at risk of infection. Always wear gardening gloves etc. Once the arm starts to swell it is unlikely to return fully to its normal state.

There was a meeting scheduled with my oncologist to discuss further treatment - he decided on 6 months chemo and 21 days of radiotherapy. I am very conscious that it all seems negative, in actual fact it wasn't exactly positive but at the time I just got on with it as anyone else would.

My chemo was to start in February and being a private patient I could have it in the comfort of my own home. Sitting here reflecting brings back the most painful memories. I was not certain what to expect but it wasn't what I got for sure. The more I think about it, my psyche reverts to what got me through the tough times and very quickly it was gaining a sense of perspective. Don't get me wrong, honestly at times I felt powerless, totally not in control of my body or mind but soon jumped back on my feet just before the next session and it would start all over again.

My psychology degree certainly served a purpose in my life. Not only did it enhance my career but it contributed to my coping mechanisms and optimistic attitude throughout this process. You will have heard it all before but it is true that the world is the same for everyone but, how each individual sees it is different. We all have a choice of how we react to experiences. We need to accept what is happening in our lives. It doesn't mean you have to resign yourself and give in. It means understand at this moment, it is what it is. Of course life brings some really difficult times which is exceptionally hard when you are suffering and you wish it was not happening but the key is to recognise you cannot change it but you can change how you deal with it.

Having a sense of perspective makes a difference between resisting or accepting the changes that are happening in your life. It gives you a sense of calm. You want things to be different in the future, but in the present moment you accept things as they are and cling on to the wonderful thought that it will soon pass.

Believe it or not it is a struggle revealing some of this stuff. Then why do it? I have never accepted that it could return and until last year made no changes to my lifestyle. Initially I was told that after five years the possibility of it returning reduces and my cancer was one of the best to have, if there is a best. Now there is evidence to say the risk of return after five years is just the same and will not reduce. This experience has made me so much stronger and more appreciative of life.

CHAPTER EIGHT

February 2012 – My first Chemo

How bad can it be? I can cope with anything

The time until my first chemo passed rapidly it was only
three weeks but the advice given to me was to build up
my strength. It was my intention not to disappoint. We
tried to carry on as normal, eating out and having
snuggly evenings on the sofa with a bottle of wine.
Whiskey the dog enjoyed long walks and I became an
established and fully-fledged member of the dog park.
Facing the house we lived in at the time was a field
which was purposely made into a dog park, where one
could take their pooch and let it run free. It was the
protocol to walk around the field only anti-clockwise
with the other dog owners chatting. Soon learning the
strict code of conduct – DO NOT let your dog pick up
another dogs ball and even worse DO NOT call the dog a
he if it is was a she and vice versa. Seriously I did meet
some really lovely people, although there was a
hierarchy and your face had to fit to be accepted.
Thankfully I was ok.

The day came and I was not bothered at all. I was
looking forward to getting the first one over with then at
least I would know what to expect. I mean really, how
bad would it be. Loads of people do it all the time. The
nurse came to the house and we had a chat about the

procedure and what to expect. I had been previously given a helmet to put in the freezer. It is a personal choice if you want to wear it whilst having your treatment, they are called cold caps. If you have your chemo in the hospital the cold cap is attached to a machine which is temperature regulated. As my treatment was from home, the cap had to be kept in the freezer, wearing it 30 mins before, during and 30 mins after. By freezing the head it narrows the blood vessels, lessening the chemotherapy reaching the hair follicles. It was so uncomfortable; as soon as the nurse arrived it had to come off. I can only cope with concentrating on one uncomfortable situation at a time. The cap would only minimise the hair loss so instead of going completely bald I would have bald patches with random strands of hair. So my decision was easy. The nurse was lovely. As stated earlier, my treatment was private so consequently I was having it at home and was made to believe this was a good thing.

The vision is clear, the nurse arrives bringing in all the equipment and setting it up beside me chatting away. We had a long conversation about what to expect and she explained every small detail. "Oh I'll be fine" I said "I am really resilient aren't I David". The nurse glared at me and told me to prepare for it not to be pleasant. It still didn't worry me. I could look up the names of the drugs but I won't because I never researched anything. I didn't want to know and didn't really care, so to me it was just a giant syringe of dark pink medicine (whenever I see rose wine now I feel sick) which was attached to a cannula. She brought the steroid medication also but I refused to take it. The reports of its affects worried me, so as much as they tried to talk me into it, I flatly refused. The drugs are so poisonous that the nurse is not allowed to carry them with her to other appointments. She is instructed to take the drugs from a locked fridge immediately before the consultation. She injected some harmless dye into my vein to ensure the vein would not leak when the chemo was inserted. Should it leak it would cause severe burns to my arm. What!!! mmm worry setting in quickly. It was soon set up and the nurse left to return when it had been fully administered. I felt fine. She advised I have a lay down and rest. David made me a sandwich and went out to the shops while I had a sleep on the sofa.

Next thing my eyes opened to David waking me on his return. Sitting up, it hit me. What was happening? I felt so dizzy and so very sick. The Loo! Where is it? Violently vomiting does not cut it. Sick does not explain it. I lay on the sofa, I lay on the floor, on the steps, in the bath, in bed and nothing could comfort me. It was awful but not the worst by a long shot. It lasted 2 to 3 days. By the 4th day I was in shock but ok. The nurse returned to take my blood only to find my body was not replenishing the blood cells. (The chemo kills the blood cells and your body has 3weeks to build them back up so the process can be repeated and this happens 6 times).
 Consequently after each session I had an injection to stimulate my bone marrow to produce blood cells.

Whilst I was having my first chemo session, my sister Pauline was having her surgery. She had a different type of cancer to me, a more aggressive sort. Mine was a grade 2, Pauline's was a grade 3 and poor Anne was a grade 4.

Pauline and I chat almost every day, she makes me laugh. We were chatting this morning on my way to work in Hull. I said "have you anything new to tell me?" she replied "no, not really... Oh I have a fab joke – why did the scarecrow win an award?" "I have no idea!!" "Because he was outstanding in the field" bum bum! Funny yes???

Anyway, it was extremely interesting that each hospital has different approaches to the whole thing. Bradford has a procedure completely different to York. We could not believe it was happening to all three of us. For poor Anne it was the worst ever. We were there for her. She was and still is an angel as she suffered so badly - I still cannot comprehend she has gone.

Back to February 2012 - In between the first and the second chemo the inevitable happened. I started to wake up in the morning with mountains of hair on my pillow. At first I decided to keep it to myself so as not to upset Georgia. I stopped brushing my hair until one day I pulled out a massive bunch and thought WTF accept it so I did - my son Chris shaved the whole lot off and I went for a fitting for my first wig. My thoughts were - I'm going big or go home - long brown wig for me please. I loved it. Over the months I tried many different wigs but my favorite was the short one, it looked the most natural. It was fabulous not to have to worry about styling my hair. It never went flat or frizzy but it did itch a tad. My neighbour who was a hairdresser would cut and style them. A good tip is to always wear a clip or a headband - it throws people off noticing it is a wig. At the time I thought they were ace but looking back at pictures they do look obvious - not so much the short one.

The second chemo session was worse than the first. The procedure was the same only this time I was talked into having the steroids. The anti-sickness tablets just weren't strong enough last time so had a stronger type. Almost to the second the sickness began only this time it got worse and as I thought, surely it can't get any worse; it answered "watch me!!!!!"

I rang my close friend Tracey, I paced the bedroom floor in between being sick, I knelt over the bed with a wet towel around my head. Anyone who has experienced it will agree it is not a normal sick. The steroids had made it so much worse - in addition to the sickness it had decided to give me a knuckle crunching headache. The sickness was not triggered from my stomach, it was from my brain. It felt like I had been spinning constantly on a fair ride for hours. I was frightened; I did not feel in control. The vomiting proceeded to get worse. There just was not a spit on my stomach to come up but that didn't matter, I could not breath. The whole house was in distress. The dog was crying and constantly by my side, David asked me if I could try and stop as everyone was getting really upset. You can imagine the language that came out of my mouth at that point. I made everyone stay downstairs and leave me alone. I just wanted to curl in a ball which is what I did – on the floor.

Then I remembered being giving me the number of the on call nurse to ring if I had any problems. I rummaged in my notes to find it. Feeling a glimmer of hope, I called. She didn't know what to say. I couldn't believe what I was experiencing. She answered the call – Thank God I thought, in fact I think I actually said it. I tried to explain what was happening but to my horror I was in competition with her screaming kids in the background arguing. Who was going to scream the loudest? Well one thing you can be certain of, trust me, it was going to be me. However, after having to repeat myself three times I accepted defeat – Hanging up I muttered "you little fuckers win!" Through my sobs I wailed "just fucking wait until I speak to my oncologist in the morning.

Do you know what? I completely forgot how bad it was until I wrote this.

The next day my objective was to make contact with the Oncologist's secretary. She arranged an appointment to see him that week. The Oncologists are very tactile and empathic in the way they communicate with you. It is part of the job I suppose. In private at the Nuffield the waiting room is very comfortable and he comes out to greet you and take you in. He would give my shoulder a gentle squeeze making me feel like a little girl. Not this time, I pounced in behind him, I meant business.
"Everything ok sweetheart, how are you feeling?"
"Don't sweetheart me" I thought but didn't say. What I did do, is proceed to tell him about my experience after the chemotherapy. I told him how angry and abandoned I felt, how I was left to cope on my own and it was not fair on my family. I couldn't get in touch with anyone and when I did, the nurse was not in a position to offer me a solution. I told him it was disgusting and I actually remember saying "is that how you feel when you are dying because if it is I am terrified".

He reassured me that should never have happened with the nurse and that I had a bad reaction to the chemo. He booked me in to the private hospital in Leeds for my next one. I am not soft by any means and have a high tolerance of most things. For me it really did not work having the chemotherapy at home; 1. Due to the reaction I had and 2. For a long time my safe home which I loved would be associated with something dark and distressing. My dressing gown and the bed sheets were thrown away as they had a smell of fear. I never wanted to see them again.

Even though positivity has always taken priority in my life, it was very challenging to view my world at this point in a positive light. The only thing you can do in a situation like this is keep searching for the light at the end of your tunnel. You may laugh but even at my lowest point when I thought I may die from this, I remember thinking well at least I haven't had to jump from the twin towers. (Months later Anne and I were having this same conversation when she was really scared of dying. I told her I was once terrified of dying and I had to try and think of a positive. She replied "for fuck sake Jane, there is nothing positive about dying". "I know" I told her - then I explained about the twin towers and she actually agreed. It made her feel the tiniest bit better but it really was a tiny bit because let's face it there is nothing positive about dying.)

Apologies to anyone reading this who may be embarking on a similar experience. I cannot flower it up - it is what it is. You will get through it and everyone's experience is different. Some people breeze through it. It affects people in many different ways. It is nothing to do with tolerance but to do with how your body reacts and copes with it.

I definitely have taken some positives from it in terms of appreciating what is important in life and you will too. I appreciate my family much more than I ever did. My husband is a really good person and I love him dearly. He really cares about me and loves me so very much.

One thing which is amazing is we still have such a laugh. Sometimes he makes me belly laugh so hard, he has a fantastic sense of humor. My family means so much to me.

Back to April 2012

This would be my third session. My girlfriends Tracey, Jackie and Linda were coming to sit with me for support as I wanted my husband to go to work and be normal. So he came and sat with me until the girls arrived. The nurses were just setting up the room as there were going to be five having treatment that day and I was the first to arrive. Each patient was allocated her own nurse to look after her/him. I can't remember the name of mine, it was different each time you went but she was lovely. After asking me what had happened for me to continue at the hospital, she was disgusted and shared something with me that was dreadful. She said that private patients were encouraged to have chemo at home as it cost the insurance companies less money. ALSO (allegedly) the oncologists were incentivised by the insurance companies to keep patients out of hospital. The oncologists would then put the nurses under pressure to do the same. I was fuming!!!! But in the words of "frozen" I let it go!!!

My memory of the surroundings are as clear as day. I felt fine, just wanted to get it over with. Desperate to show my friends how brave I was. Jackie and Linda came and sat beside me. Tracey came a little later when she finished work.

Fifth chair along was a young woman in her 40s having the cold cap. It was her first session and she had lovely long blonde hair. I remember thinking please let it work, she has such beautiful hair - by the third session she had given up and unfortunately she lost her hair just like the rest of us.

The girls and I were chatting as you do and all was fine until the nurse tried to insert the needle for the chemo. To cut a long story short my veins had collapsed and she couldn't get the needle in. It was very painful - I broke down - not because of the pain but I felt out of control. It had to be done so she had to force it in. My friends were there at the right time and Jackie fell immediately into the role of nursing - caring - calming and really she softly talked me through the next half hour. She knew exactly what to do and say to comfort me.

The nurse advised me that my veins would not stand another session so she rang the surgeon there and then. She booked me in for a portal to be inserted under my skin on my chest with a tube linking to the vein in my neck. This would be used to insert the needles in the future. Yeay!!! I'll look forward to that.

After the chemo was done I was led upstairs with the girls to my hospital room. I put on my jams, sat on the bed and we chatted over coffee. Every little twinge I was waiting for the headache and sickness to begin. Sure enough it did. I could feel it coming, swirling around in my head. Starting to pace the room, the girls were trying to comfort me but I just wanted to be alone. The nurse came in. Everything and everyone was making me angry. I pulled off my wig in frustration - forgetting the girls were in the room - I think they were shocked to see me bald. Tracey left the room which made me grasp how upsetting it was for them. Suggesting it would be better for them to go - we hugged and they left.

Things got worse and no matter what the nurse gave me I could not stop vomiting. It got to midnight and she had to call in the oncologist (not my regular one). He was so kind and lovely. He put me on a syringe driver which stopped the sickness but knocked me out for two days. I just kept waking up when my meals were brought in but fell back asleep before I could eat them. It did wonders for the diet. There were periods of time when I would not be asleep but unable to move. Such a strange sensation being aware of my surroundings but unable to move my limbs, like my body was asleep but my mind alert. What could I do other than daydream thinking about the good times? I would just lay there thinking about events good and bad that had happened to me over the years. My mind wandered from one thing to another. Did I actually do that? What made me say that? What has happened to her/him? What are they doing right now while I am laying here thinking?

A friend who has been reading this manuscript asked me why would I be thinking about partying – why wasn't I thinking about my family? Fair point! However there is a reason for this. I was thinking about my family, special times we had together and how much I loved them but these thoughts upset me, forcing me into a state of anxiety knowing how worried they were, so I forced myself to think of something remotely removed from my emotions.

Why had I taken for granted the fab places I had been to with my job - Dubai - Italy - Egypt - USA - parties on the beach - party by moonlight at the bottom of the pyramids - totally incredible. We also had some amazing experiences with David's job. He once ran the Mercedes Benz dealership in Manchester and often held events. David Beckham amongst others bought a car from him - I mean of course they weren't mates but they were quite friendly and he would attend any of the events at the garage. At one of the events, Beckham came with Brooklyn - he was about two years old - I had to look after him in the office. We chatted for ages and he gave my son Christopher a signed England shirt. We were once using his car and I found a love letter in the glove box to posh spice. My husband had a hissy fit and made me put it back. He gave us free tickets to the Man U games and we were invited to the players bar afterwards. This is ME - Jane from the council estate. There was a crowd of us at the England/Greece game when Beckham scored the famous goal - the atmosphere was astounding. Afterwards bar hopping in Manchester amongst the players. Another time we were invited to the OK magazine charity ball - all the Man U players were there. I was sat next to Carol Vorderman, Gary Neville and Neville Neville, his father who never stopped chatting - we had such a laugh. By the end of the night I was very tipsy. I was breaking my moves on the dance floor with one of the other wives (we clicked completely). She said "Jane, Teddy can't take his eyes off you". I couldn't believe it. I was trying so hard to do my best sassy dance, then I realised I had been to the loo and not pulled down the inside of my dress, exposing my knickers to the world and the footballer. My immediate thoughts were towards the stupid decision not to wear my sexy thong - instead I chose the Spanx which pulled right up under my armpits. I was mortified - he laughed, picked me up and carried me to the loo.

After a few years with Mercedes he moved position to Leeds and was in charge of the Porsche and Ferrari Dealership Which brought a whole set of new experiences. Those were the days.

Now I was waiting to go home and recover before the next session.

CHAPTER NINE

A cat with 9 lives

This week alone - over 250 women in the UK will die of breast cancer

Approx. 350 men develop breast cancer in the UK every year and about 90 will die

One in seven women never check their breasts and 25% of them are over 50

You should check your breast once a month, always at the same time every month

For women the lifetime risk of being diagnosed is 1 in 9

I arrived at the spire private hospital in Leeds for the fitting of my Portal. Going through the usual procedures before an op, the nurse came to take me down to theatre. I had done this so many times now it was just another day but for some reason this time I had a melt down and for me this is a difficult thing to say but fear set in. By the time theatre was visible I was in a state. As you would imagine everyone was lovely and tried to console me. This particular procedure had to be done under local anesthetic with a sedative. A round hard portal the size of a 2p put under my skin just above my breast with a tube connecting to a vein in my neck. "Please just put me to sleep" I bawled "I'm not supposed to" He replied but the next thing I knew I was waking up in recovery and it was all over.

The nurse forgot to give me my numbing cream to go home with so my advice to anyone is make sure you don't forget it that's all I will say. I made sure I had plenty in the fridge after my first injection without. I think I actually told the nurse to fuck off the next day when she tried to take blood. She said she didn't blame me as she had no numbing cream and the blood had to be taken. That was another challenge dealt with – tick. Now I could have all my injections from the portal including my chemo which was great.

My girlfriends very kindly took me away for a few days to Robin Hoods Bay in a very small, gorgeous fisherman's cottage. It was beautiful and they did everything for me, all I had to do was relax. Thank you Tracey, Jackie and Linda!!!! We drank, we ate, we laughed, walked on the beach and watched movies in front of a roaring fire.

Before the blink of an eye I was back for my next session. I could not keep my eyes open when the chemo was over I fell fast asleep in the chair. They put me in a wheelchair and took me to my room for my syringe driver and once again I lay for two days sleeping and when I wasn't sleeping I was laid there not being able to move just thinking.

I am undeniably a cat with 9 lives, losing my first life when I was two. It was another day carved in my memory. My oldest recollection was waking up on my dad's knee in the back of a car. I looked down and saw my bone sticking out through the skin on my leg. It was the day of the May procession at St Winifred's church, Wibsey. My sister, Pauline had taken me to her friends over the field outside the house. To cut a long story short I ran out between two parked cars and was hit by a Mercedes. I broke my legs, my pelvis and fractured my scull. How did I survive? Because I'm a tough cookie, that's why. My dad wouldn't wait for the ambulance and took me to hospital in the car.   My parents were told it was possible I wouldn't ever be able to walk again because of my pelvis. I was in hospital a couple of months and remember my parents visiting me every evening for half an hour because that was all they were allowed. Every evening my mum would bring me my dummy and pluckie (a blanket I would pluck) and every night the nurse would take them off me and put them in the bin. Heartless bitch!!!!

Anyway eventually I learned to walk again - just so I could cause more worry to my parents because that's what kids do!!! It made me very insecure as a child and was attached to my mother's hip 24/7. It is a mystery to me how growing up my mother and I became distant when I relied on her so much as a child.

TIME (present day)

As you can imagine TIME is very precious to me. You can't go back - you can't stop it and you can't save time for another day. So I want to make every second - every day count. The last few months have been a fight against time. The days are going too quick and I need to slow them right down. This happens quite often and I deal with it by consciously practicing mindfulness. Stop for a moment, right now!!!! Look around you - your surroundings and appreciate the moment.

The age thing keeps cropping up too but I still feel so young. I'm sure I heard somewhere 50 is the new 30!!!! My son Christopher once said to me "just imagine you are 80 and someone has said they can take years off you and make you the age you are now - how fab would you feel?? It really works!!!

BACK To JUNE 2012

This was my last session. It had passed pretty quickly and it was encouraging to know my life could start getting back to normal. In no time at all I was in my room at the hospital settling down to rest. My little routine was working well - before the syringe driver kicked in I would ring around everyone and catch up on what had happened that day in the normal world. My sister Anne had been put on a new drug for her cancer. The idea was it would shrink the tumor but the medication was making her too ill so she had to come off it which was devastating news. I lay again thinking of my nine lives and thank god I have survived them. The nurse came in to check the syringe driver and I drifted off casting my mind back to FEBRUARY 2004.

I had been a drugs rep for 2 years and just returned from conference full of enthusiasm. It was a lovely day for February and I had promised to take my daughter shopping for shoes, she was 7. As the kids were still quite young, I worked part time and finished at 1. This particular day I was in Knaresborough doing an educational lunch meeting on a particular anti-depressant. I remember I had laid the lunch out in the meeting room and was waiting for the Health Care Professionals to arrive - they were running late but eventually turned up and I presented to them whilst they ate. I quickly packed up and left as I wanted to drive home, get things sorted before I picked up Georgia from school.

I distinctly remember driving down the a59, listening to my music. There were a couple of cars behind me but in front it was clear apart from the oncoming traffic. A white transit van was in the distance on the other side of the road and I remember thinking it was going too fast - in the blink of an eye there was something unusual coming towards me. It was all literally in two seconds - I knew it wasn't a car and it shouldn't be there - it was racing straight for me on my side of the road. The van was pulling a massive trailer with road marking equipment and gas bottles weighing over a ton and the driver had forgot to put the securing pins in to secure it to the van and as he sped down the road, it detached from the van and hit me head on at 60mph

CHAPTER TEN

This is going to really hurt!!!!!

Gripping the steering wheel tight, my whole body immediately tensed to welcome the impact. There was an almighty explosion that rang through my head from ear to ear. After blacking out, my eyes opened to a man at the side of me looking in horror through the window. "She's alive!" pandemonium set in. There were people running around panicking. My instant concerns were of the intense icy cold feeling all over my body, like I had been dipped in an ice bucket. Shaking from head to foot, looking around in shock and slow motion I became aware of my surroundings. The windscreen was smashed and to the right of me, a gas bottle half in and half out of the windscreen. To the left of me a man shouting something to me but I couldn't quite hear him, everything was muffled. Sheer panic set in. A woman opened the passenger door and sat beside me. "Don't panic" she said "I am a nurse and I am going to help you through this - help is on its way and I just want you to keep calm" even though the car was crushed, the engine was still running. My arm and elbow were badly broken but survival took over and I used it to switch the engine off.

It didn't seem too long before the ambulance and fire rescue arrived. By this time I had got a grip of myself. It felt surreal, like having an out of body experience just watching it all happening from above. I took a moment to be mindful of my surroundings - fire, police, ambulance, road closed, a crowd of people and cars as far as the eye could see. After being informed that they would have to use equipment to cut me free, two fire officers straight out of the Chippendales were assigned to look after me. One swapped places with the nurse at one side and the other leaned through the window at the other. After all that was happening, the banter started. Well, it would have been rude not to!!!!

The fireman to my right, leaning in the window was staring at my feet. Immediately I bellowed "what?" "Why are you looking at my feet" he looked at me and smiled "I'm not! I was just thinking what lovely pins you have" I smiled back knowing he had no interest in my lovely pins.

Eventually the side of the car was taken off and I was carefully lifted out of the car onto a stretcher and put into the ambulance. The paramedic did all what she was supposed to do and on the way to the hospital announced she was going to attempt to remove my boot which she did and informed me my leg was a mess, a terrible mess. I was shocked as I couldn't really feel it. My body was in so much shock. "How bad is it" I asked. "Very bad" she replied. Proceeding to ask questions, her replies led to the possibility of me losing my foot.

The trailer that hit me had a severed metal bar which penetrated straight through my car, my thick leather boot and straight through my lower leg. Obviously tearing my leg open and snapping my leg in half at the ankle. Fucking ouch!!!!

In my darkest moments I have reflected back to past experiences good and bad. Our experiences in life determine who we are and how we cope with the here and now.

Initially I was treated by the NHS and was placed on the trauma ward with three elderly patients who had hip replacements. Very frightened and treat poorly. Not the nurses fault as they were severely understaffed but I was left unwashed with glass in my hair. One evening a foreign registrar came to see me in the middle of the night and said he needed to examine my breasts. I flatly refused and said it was my neck that hurt not my breasts. I never saw him again – weird. After 4 days I was moved to private where 3 nurses looked after me every minute of the day. My ankle was operated on 3 times and to save the skin I had to keep my leg still and elevated for 3 months after. The screws are still in there. The wound was horrendous and would not heal - it had to be cleaned and dressed daily for two months facing numerous infections. My arm was crushed like a biscuit and it took an 8 hour op to piece it together with rods and glue. The prognosis for me being able to have normal function with my arm and leg was very poor. Thankfully working tirelessly for months, even years on strengthening them, I now have normal usage with both. I have a scar on my ankle which truly resembles a shark bite. It is not pretty; however to me it is beautiful and makes me unique. It has never ever bothered me. It is part of who I am.

It is necessary I tell you of the massive crush I had on my Surgeon. He was bloody gorgeous! We had a great rapport. He would come on the ward to see me at the weekends and bring his kids. He really cared about me and I found it very difficult when after 6 months I was discharged. It was like ending a relationship purely because I depended on him for my recovery. David knew and we laughed about it. He would say "Jane' do you think he'd fancy you when he has operated on you with your catheter in, you more than likely farted in his face" I just laughed because it was probably true!!!!!!!!

Now I know what you are thinking, this book is meant to be about the breast cancer; however, these are the experiences that have made me who I am today. They have made me the positive strong woman that I am proud to be. These are the experiences that have made me value life, love life, respect life and cope with whatever life throws at me. These are the experiences that have enabled me to stand up to the cancer that over the years has executed my family one by one.

CHAPTER ELEVEN

P Diddy was spinning the tunes

Sometime later the pins had to be taken out of my arm which was an enormous relief as the pain they caused was unbearable. The surgery went to plan and two weeks after that was my follow up appointment. I remember it as clear as day. It was the day before David and I were going on a trip with his work. At the time my husband was a Dealer Principle for two Porsche dealerships and a Ferrari/Maserati/Lotus dealership - big job, big money, massive pressure anyway that's another story. The trip was - wait for it! VIP guests at the Grand Prix Monaco Ferrari stand!!!!! I look back now and think WTF but then I didn't appreciate it as much as I should have. . Anyway I was having my follow up appointment with Dr Dreamy. He gathered all his registrars and nurses around to see the fantastic results with the skin on my ankle and told them in envy where I was going the next day.

The rationality for my husband and I embarking on this trip was to host four other couples (Ferrari owners) who had paid thousands for the privilege. The other couples were lovely - I am still close friends with one of the wives. Two couples our age one of which an Indian couple and the rest a little older. We all immediately bonded and began to have a lot of fun laughing and joking, drinking and shopping.

The first evening we went to the casino and to the bars on the strip - they were packed with racing drivers, the crew and TV presenters. Honestly words do not do it justice as to how fantastic the atmosphere was. Dancing outside the bars, champagne on tap. In one of the bars there were wooden tables and in a split second the girls were pulled up onto the tables to dance. The Indian girl was so very funny. The heat was stifling and the atmosphere electric - packed to the brim with money yet all class destroyed - we were dancing to I'm a believer by the monkeys, still on the table top, I glanced across the room above all the heads of the non-table dancers and spotted a female drag a guy by the hand into the loo. I mean it was carnage. The Indian girl was hell bent on losing her husband accidentally on purpose. "I can't" I told her "David will kill me". I looked across the room to David and yes he was piercing me with his eyes as if to say behave yourself!!! The night was amazing fun and the next day, in my opinion, boring watching the racing so the Indian girl, the tennis player (one of the other wives) and I explored, mingled and shopped. They were really good fun to be with.

The tennis player mentioned that a guy who she was close with at university was now a film producer and he was at the Cannes film festival. She had spoken to him and he could get us into Naomi Campbell's birthday party on the beach. Yeah right I thought - how shocked was I because it was true. The next night we all went into Cannes, it was amazing and yes we did get into the party and P Diddy was the DJ. It was nothing short of surreal and incredibly exciting. We didn't see Naomi there but did see her the next evening. I could really elaborate on the events but trying to keep it brief.

The next evening was interesting to say the least. Remember the film producer? Well, he was having a party on a yacht and anyone worth knowing was going to be there. The tennis player and the Indian girl were hell bent on attending. I mean it would have been rude not to don't you think? There was only one problem – we weren't invited. The ploy was ME. He had taken a liking to me so they decided I had to work him to get us all an invite. "You will have to OK it with David" I said with trepidation. "Please Jane, we have a very small chance of getting to that party and you are our slim chance" "Don't hold out much hope" I replied with a worried desperate look that said HELP! "You will have to ask David if he minds, as I am not asking him" They did and he wasn't too happy but agreed to me just chatting to him and trying to get us an invite. WELL - believe me I tried and I tried and my enthusiasm was deteriorating whilst my champagne flute was constantly being replenished. As the minutes turned into hours I got sick of trying and to be quite frank he was getting on my nerves. It wasn't fun anymore, he was boring and there was no way he was letting us on - so we shook him off and walked to the club.

The streets were crowded with crazy individuals moving in all directions. Some in party gear with all the glitz and others in ripped jeans and pumps but still looking awesome and menacingly rich.

We arrived at what looked like the place to be and positioned ourselves discreetly and orderly in the queue. After waiting patiently, chatting and soaking up the atmosphere, the doorman began to allow the queue to enter, inspecting each individual as they passed him. We had no idea at the time but in front of the Indian girl discretely in the orderly queue were Tamara Beckwith, Amanda Holden and a few other women. The doorman assumed we were with them and stopped the rest of the group entering. We were pulled along with the others into the club to an atmosphere that was something I have never experienced before. Amanda Holden grabbed my wrist and pulled me onto the dance floor. We were all jumping around laughing. The Indian girl screeched in my ear "we have made it" at that point a glass of champagne was thrust into my hand and I proceeded to do what any other sane woman in position would do – I necked it in one "Jane, please just let's enjoy it". At that moment I glanced to the window where the others were (the whole of the front of the club was a window) I could just make out what David was saying "get your fucking arse out here Jane". Who could blame him, we were the hosts. "I have to leave" I had to say through gritted teeth. She reluctantly followed me passing the ladies loo, Naomi Campbell came rushing out almost tripping over me. Grabbing my hand she pulled me into the men's and asked me to hold the toilet door while she had a pee. Of course I obliged and when she had done, smacked a kiss on my cheek and said thank you.

We joined the rest of the group, accepted with grace the sarcastic comments and proceeded along the strip to a bar where we all sat in a group at a table outside. The film producer appeared out of nowhere and joined the group for a drink. The trip continued to be exciting. I know it sounds unbelievable and it is not an excuse to name drop – it was a tool I called upon whilst laid on my hospital bed feeling like shit, looking like shit and in need of escape.

CHAPTER TWELVE

Difficult choices

Tamoxifen

18th October 2016

The heading for this page is based on some very sad news received yesterday. Not only sad but extremely worrying regarding the choices we are given when faced with breast cancer. Some make their choices on an emotional state of mind based on where their life is at that particular moment. This mirrors my belief in mindfulness. However there are certain situations which advocate looking at the bigger picture. I hope that makes sense and it will become clear. Also today is the anniversary of my lovely sister who passed with breast cancer aged 34 in 1988.

When I was diagnosed with breast cancer, a friend of my sister who is 15 years younger than me was also diagnosed with the same type. As we all are, she was given a choice as to her treatment. She was young and in a newish relationship so as you can imagine the thought of a mastectomy was devastating and terrifying for her. She chose the option of radiotherapy first to shrink the tumor and then to have the lump removed - to finish off with chemo. Well the bastard returned this year and now she has only 3 months to live. I cannot comprehend how you deal with that news even though I have lived through it with my sisters and parents. We all have our own reasons for the choices we make in life but please think hard about what could potentially happen in the future. Consider the risks verses the benefits. I had no hesitation what so ever when I was diagnosed. I didn't even think about it "take them both off" I said. That was an extremely difficult but easy statement to make. My breasts were my greatest assets. Even though I had breastfed two children I had fantastic big firm breasts BUT I had watched my sister take her last breath as a result of this terrible disease and it was vital to minimise the risk of it happening to me.

Returning to edit this chapter the poor girl I mentioned has now passed away.

Lest get back to the breast cancer
From the Jeremy vine show/Radio 2 - 9th November 2017

There is a new study which shows breast cancer has a high risk of returning up to 15 years after successful treatment. Researchers from the University of Oxford found that those who take anticancer medication for five years remain at a similar risk for up to 15 years. This disturbingly begs the question "are we really all clear after 5?" Prof Richard Grey from the Nuffield was lead author on the report.

Three quarters of women have hormone sensitive tumors and progress to take Tamoxifen for 5 years after treatment which cuts the risk of reoccurrence by 50%.

We assumed that after the 5 years the risk of cancer returning diminishes as time goes on but in actual fact it continues at the same rate of reoccurrence as in the 5 years. The risk of reoccurrence depends on if the cancer had spread to the lymph nodes. Even the best group of cancer with the lowest risk had a 15% chance of it coming back over the 15 years. For those with the worst outlook the risk was as high as 40%. (The worst outlook would be having a larger tumor and it spreading to more lymph nodes).

The study was done to see if it was beneficial to carry on with Tamoxifen after 5 years. Tamoxifen has side effects such as weight gain, tiredness and hot flushes but you have to weigh up the risks v benefits and the benefits are that it reduces the risk of reoccurrence significantly by carrying on the treatment after the 5 years. The % risk be it the 15% or 40% stays the same even after 15 years – it does not decrease as the years go by.

The cancer without the hormone sensitivity surprisingly has a much lower risk of reoccurrence as time goes on. They looked at other factors like diet, exercise and stress but they had very little effect the main factors for reoccurrence was like I said earlier, the size of the tumor and if it had spread to the lymph nodes. Prof Grey believed it is possible the reoccurring cancer could have lain dormant somewhere in the body and something would trigger it off to start the cancer up again.

CHAPTER THIRTEEN

Cherry Blossom

Three weeks after my chemo finished I started my radiotherapy. I was booked in for three solid weeks - that's every day at Jimmy's in Leeds. Really, it wasn't too bad. In fact it was a breeze compared to chemo. Anyone who has experienced this will know you have to be measured up first. I can't really explain it but the area they blast with radiotherapy had to be measured exact and marked out with tattoos which are dots so that each daily treatment is easily positioned within the marked areas. One of the dots is right between my new lovely breasts. In my fifth year in remission I had it covered up with a tattoo of a cherry blossom to mark how my life has blossomed and how I continue to grow as a person day by day.

The only drawback for me with the radiotherapy was the fatigue. It was immense. I fought it but it fought back harder. You don't realise how hard it hits you until you try to forget and be normal. One of my friends was having a 70s fancy dress party at her house - I decided to go as a schoolgirl being that I actually was a schoolgirl in the 70s. Wearing one of my wigs styled with two cute pig tails, I appreciated the introduction back into socialising with friends. Not being permitted to drink didn't matter to me as the feeling of freedom and fun was intoxicating in itself. However, half way through the evening the fatigue hit me. A feeling of total exhaustion engulfed my being. Trying not to draw attention to myself or disturb anyone, I took myself out of the crowd, laid on a bench outside and fell fast asleep waking to find a couple of people helping me up - I had no wig on and was led through the crowd to bed with my very attractive bald head on display. I think I slept for three days to get over it.

The three weeks of Radiotherapy soon passed with very little drama. In fact it became enjoyable going every day. I would meet my sisters there for lunch. Anne was on treatment and Pauline was having her chemo so it was a time when we were clinging onto each other for support.

On my last day of radiotherapy I was given my medication, Tamoxifen which I had to now take for five years.

I couldn't have got through the next few months without my family and close friends. I thank my kids Georgia and Chris for not letting it stop them from just being kids, for walking the dog and making me cups of tea. I wouldn't have wanted them to be anything other than teenagers wrapped up in their teenage world. I thank my husband David for being amazing and giving me the closeness and love when I needed it most. For coming out of his comfort zone and dealing so brilliantly with the situation and at times for being my carer. I love you ❤. My brother Bernard for being there when I needed him, my sisters Anne and Pauline for being my guardian angels -

for showing me that life is a gift and whatever life throws at you, what differences you have had over the years, sisterly love is a love that accepts you just the way you are. Every time we were together it was like coming home. You were always there for me when I couldn't be there for myself. I loved you yesterday, I love you still, I always have and I always will.

My girlfriends Jackie, Tracey and Linda for sitting by my side that time, you remember. Thanks Jackie for talking so softly to me when I was in a mad panic and very tearful. Thanks Tracey - for being at the other end of the phone 24/7. For listening to me when I was in the pits of despair and didn't want to worry my family. Thank you girls for all your lovely cards, gifts and for taking me away to the cottage in Robin Hoods Bay and Northumberland. One thing I have learnt is family and friends are worth their weight in gold.

CHAPTER FOURTEEN
How fate deals its cards

Raise your glass of sherry to toast an exceptionally wonderful sister

This chapter is about my dear sister Anne and the last part of her life. It truly ripped my heart out watching my sister deteriorate. Whilst my health improved day by day, hers declined and crumbled. It was unbearable and unjust. I was ashamed to be surviving.

The day after my last session of radiotherapy I returned to work. So desperate to get back to normality, I returned wearing a wig as my hair had not even begun to grow back. It didn't worry me at all being so elated to be entering into the world of normality. No one even battered an eyelid. It always looked good with a clip or a plaited headband, never having to bother about it going frizzy in the fog or flat in the rain, I loved it. At this point Anne was going through a trial on a new drug that unfortunately did not work for her and she had to withdraw. However, she was up and about and fully functioning. Regrettably it was at this time she began to deteriorate. The downside for me was that I lived 40 miles away, a 2 hour round trip and was working full time. As luck would have it, Pauline lived around the corner – she visited Anne every day and was marvelous, totally amazing. I would get across to see Anne twice a week and speak to her on the phone every day.

It is more difficult for me to talk about Anne than anything I have previously shared but I need to do it, I need to express this pain. How can I explain it? Right now I feel my heart is tightening as I think about her and her suffering. It is unbearable. Her family will have their own vision and their own experience. The following is just my experience, my thoughts and feelings and my pain, my guilt, my loss. I have witnessed suffering with Bernadette and my parents which was no less a loss or experience of grief. However with Anne it was no worse, just different. Maybe it was worse. It could have been any one of us to be the unlucky one which made it so much tougher to watch Anne deteriorate and be so afraid of what was to come. Poor Anne I can't cope with it, we can't cope with it - both Pauline and I most often bring the traumatic series of events into conversation. We have to talk to each other about it because we are struggling to comprehend the brutal and heroic way Anne fought to live. She was terrified. One of my favorite songs was true colours by Cindi Lauper. I now find it difficult to listen to this which I had as my ringtone for years. When Anne was very ill she heard my phone ring, it terrified her as it made her think of death so I immediately deleted it. I just wanted to take the suffering and fear away from her.

The mental torture Anne experienced was way beyond you could imagine. Because of the cancer her lymph nodes stopped working and she uncontrollably began to retain water. It was literally seeping out of her pores. I would take my foot bath and give her foot and leg massages. We would watch the Oscar Pistorius live trial and discuss it until the cows came home. It kind of went on like that for months. She had a bed in the living room but would not get into it even during the night. She preferred to stay in the chair upright for fear of her lungs filling with water and drowning. In August 2014, I received a phone call whilst I was working to say Anne was deteriorating and had agreed to get into the bed. At that point I knew the outcome was not going to be good. Speaking to my manager at work, I explained I had a bad feeling and needed to take some time off to be with her. Packing a few things I drove across to spend the next couple of nights at her side.

Things were discussed and events happened in my absence – the following is my account and my experience only.

When I arrived, there were a few things going on, conversations, nurses, worried faces. Pauline was sat on the sofa and Anne was sat up in bed. We had a really tight hug, kiss and a cup of tea. We talked about general things and watched TV together. In the evening the three of us shared a bottle of sherry. That was her thing. For once due to not driving home, I could share a glass with them. Yes, a small glass of sherry which was my mother's favorite tipple. It really was like coming home. Anne was very tired and fell asleep so I bedded down beside her on the sofa.

When I woke the next morning there was an eerie atmosphere in the air. Opening my eyes, the sun rays were shining through the curtains. It felt warm and cozy under the duvet. Glancing over to Anne I could see she was sleeping, however, her head was shaking so I crept from the sofa and whispered to her. "Anne, Anne are you awake? Would you like a cup of tea?" She opened her eyes and looked at me. My expectations were that Anne would live up to her reputation and answer me in a fun bubbly way, but no, that was not going to happen today or ever again. She was mumbling, incoherent, not making any sense, looking at me like she had no idea who I was. Dashing from her side, I shouted her husband. I am going to be totally honest and say I can only remember bits from that day. It was a disturbing, painful day for everyone. Nurses came and went, her boys came – that is all I can remember. As the day turned to evening which is when the turn of events became inscribed in my mind forever. We were told that Anne could be like this for a few days but for some reason we knew that was not the case. I suggested her boys come and have a sleep over knowing Anne needed people around her in times of distress, especially her family. Everyone came that evening, her boys and their partners, my brother and his partner. It was a surreal situation. We were all in the living room talking about our lives growing up. The nurse came to administer a syringe driver and asked Anne if she felt anxious. I found that such a profound statement. Death was something they dealt with on a daily basis; they knew she was in her last hours. Anne nodded; they needn't have asked the question as the look on her face gave them the answer. The nurse gave her something to calm her anxiety and settled her into her bed, propped up with pillows at her request. Pauline suggested we have our glass of sherry with Anne whilst she was awake. Distressed to learn we had polished the bottle off the night before, we dashed to Tesco to buy another bottle, returning to discover Anne had drifted into a sleep. Nonetheless she was very much aware of what was going on around her. I knew this due to sitting on the bed at the side of her, whispering into her ear to squeeze my hand if she could hear me and to my delight she gently squeezed it. The talking around me was muffled as I zoned in to the love between my sister and I. Knowing my much-loved sister could hear and understand my every word, I proceeded to tell her how much I loved her and how she had been the most wonderful sister and even more wonderful mother, wife and grandma. Tenderly whispering for her to try and relax, speak softly I explained that she was surrounded by all who loved her and asked if she would like some sherry. Anne softly squeezed my hand so we proceeded to dab sherry on her lips, she instantly licked them and my heart fluttered.

My brother left with his partner and the rest of us bedded down for the evening. Her boys and their partners on the floor, I was on the sofa beside her and Pauline continued to sit on a chair at her side. We were going to take turns to sit with her. Anne had been sleeping with the lamp on most nights but for some reason that night we decided to be in darkness. Why did we do that? Nodding off for about 20 minutes, I woke to Pauline shaking me "Jane she isn't breathing, she's stopped breathing" For a few moments I was totally disorientated. It was pitch black, we were both panicking. I stumbled across the room for the light which presented the saddest, most heartbreaking vison I have ever had to encounter. Anne's arm was reaching out and her face showed sheer determination to fight for her last breath. It was a vision that will be carved into my memory until the end of time. We woke the rest of the room and what proceeded was distressing for everyone.

I would like to finish this chapter discussing with you what a wonderful person Anne was. She was such a great mother to her boys and she was incredibly proud of each one of them. To say she was funny is an understatement. Where ever, whatever Anne was involved in, you would be guaranteed to laugh your socks off. Yes, she could be feisty and so very direct but I respected that about her because you always knew where you stood. Once again a piece of my security blanket has been taken away. I came to terms with Bernadette, Mum and Dad but for some reason losing Anne is extremely challenging. Pauline and I are like two little kids really, clinging onto each other. I can't fathom out where she is. One second she was here and the next gone forever.

How fate deals its cards – we were all ill together and the only positive was that it entitled us to spend quality time with each other.

I will always miss and love you Anne.

CHAPTER FIFTEEN

My promise to Little Dolly

Dolly was my mother in law. Even though no one could ever replace my mother, Dolly came a close second and was always a mother figure to me. She expressed to everyone I was like a daughter to her. What I am trying to say is we had such a close bond. Over time we certainly grew close but never as close as her last few years. She spent a considerable amount of time staying at our family home which had four bedrooms to accommodate her needs and as mentioned in an earlier chapter, one day she just never went home. Being an equally important member of the family, Dolly fit in to our family routine with ease. I loved having her with us. The home was happy, busy and she helped with the chores as much as she could. We shopped together, chatted over endless cups of tea and she was always around creating a warm and inviting atmosphere. Even when Dolly was in her 80s, she took care in her appearance with the best creams and make up on the market and paid top prices for her clothes. She was a lovely, caring, funny lady.

Over a couple of years Dolly presented with various heartbreaking indications to her and to my husband that Dementia was on the horizon. It progressively intensified and Dolly deteriorated fast until she unfortunately had to be placed in a home. We visited numerous homes before we decided on one for her. She was such a sweetheart and everyone at the nursing home absolutely loved her. We had to choose one that was secure and we were reassured she would be safe. We left her on the Saturday afternoon after settling her in to a lovely room. There were digital combinations on every door and we felt really happy leaving her there. I had bought pictures and cushions and throws etc. An hour later we got a phone call saying Dolly had escaped and the police were out looking for her. She had waited at the door and when a visitor left she followed them out and walked two miles to the village in her slippers. How did she manage that!!! We couldn't even get out - we had to ask someone the combination twice but Dolly never stuck fast she was on a mission.

The police picked her up and brought her back to a more secure home where one of the girls was waiting for her called Joanne. From that moment on they were inseparable. I loved going to see her - she waited for me and would show me off to everyone. One time she was convinced she was a movie star and had a big red sports car with a queue of reporters waiting for an interview. How fab was that? I tell ya – if I ever have dementia, I want to be in that world.

Christmas Eve, December 2014, Georgia and I stayed up watching a movie and at midnight decided to take whiskey, our pooch for a walk. It was lovely and we walked to the fields passing groups of people coming out of the pub wishing us a merry Christmas. When we returned home we were wide awake so I suggested we go to see grandma (Dolly) at the home (by this time it was 1am). I had the combination to get in as it was my second home and knew she was always up at night. We took her gifts and a picnic and couldn't wait to surprise her. Georgia and I creeped quietly into the home and arrived outside her bedroom door to hear her scream "get off me! Leave me alone" I stormed into her room to find some big woman manhandling her. I was fuming to say the least - they hadn't contacted me as didn't want to spoil our Christmas Eve (we were going to see her Christmas Day) "get off her" I shouted "get out and get me the manager now!" It was very upsetting. I rushed to her side and she looked so happy to see me "please don't leave me" she cried "never" I replied "Dolly I am here and I will not leave your side".

The manager came and I was furious explaining the situation. She tried to reassure me that the woman was doing her job – She was sacked two weeks later. I knew poor Dolly was not in a good way and the manager informed me she had pneumonia. "I will now look after her and attend to her needs". I climbed into bed next to her and held her in my arms, until she died on Boxing Day. Of course it was heartbreaking; however having Dolly die in my arms wasn't frightening or disturbing. It was an extremely beautiful, emotional sensation. Knowing I was with her, comforting her just as I promised I would.

CHAPTER SIXTEEN

Medications

This chapter will look at the medications which have assisted me with my recovery. I will explain top line about the specific medication and my personal opinions. I am obviously not medically qualified to make medical decisions or give advice, so please seek guidance from your GP or nurse before taking any medication or vitamin.

Tamoxifen

Tamoxifen will only be prescribed if your breast cancer has receptors within the cell that bind to the hormone oestrogen (known as oestrogen receptor positive or ER+ breast cancer). It works on the whole body (known as systemic treatment) and blocks the effects of oestrogen on the receptors. This helps to stop any breast cancer cells from growing.

Tamoxifen can be used for primary breast cancer as additional treatment following surgery, to reduce the risk of the cancer coming back and to reduce the risk of a new breast cancer developing. If you are going to take Tamoxifen as part of your treatment for primary breast cancer, your specialist will tell you when is best for you to do this.

Tamoxifen may be an option for some people who have a high risk of developing breast cancer because of a significant family history. It is given to try to reduce the risk of breast cancer developing.

All side effects for any drug by law have to be displayed on the patient information leaflet. My personal experience with Tamoxifen is as follows: I was advised to take Tamoxifen once a day for a period of five years. I chose not to research it or read any forums that would put the thought of a side effect in my mind. However the immediate effect for me was weight gain (well it was never going to be my luck that it would make me lose lots of weight). I did not eat any differently, however within a month I gained a stone of which some thankfully, with a lot of effort reduced over the five years. Other side effects were obviously the hot flushes, especially at night, bone pain and the chronic fatigue. I am extremely pleased to say the only side effects now for me are very mild hot flushes and occasional muscle pain. So in my experience the side effects are transient. I quickly discovered that I tolerated TEVA brand much better than any of the others so I had it put on my repeat prescription 'TEVA brand only'.

Anastrozole

A study named ATAC provided results that found Anastrozole was more effective than Tamoxifen in reducing the risk of recurrence of early-stage, hormone-receptor-positive breast cancer in postmenopausal women. Other studies comparing Tamoxifen to the other two aromatase inhibitors (Aromasin and Femara) have shown similar results.3 Oct 2010

After 10 years of follow-up, a study shows that taking Anastrozole (Arimidex) for 5 years is better at reducing the risk of hormone-receptor-positive breast cancer recurrence than taking Tamoxifen for 5 years. These results were presented at the 2010 American Society of Clinical Oncology (ASCO) Breast Cancer Symposium.

Five years after diagnosis:

- 9.8% of women who took Anastrozole for 5 years had a recurrence
- 12.5% of women who took Tamoxifen for 5 years had a recurrence

Ten years after diagnosis:

- 19.7% of women who took Anastrozole for 5 years had a recurrence
- 24% of women who took Tamoxifen for 5 years had a recurrence

This means that women taking Anastrozole after surgery and other treatments were 21% less likely than women taking Tamoxifen to have a recurrence over 10 years (5 years after finishing hormonal therapy treatment).

Vitamin D

Over the 5 years, I frequented my GP surgery on an embarrassing scale. The chronic fatigue was having such a soul destroying effect on my life that at times I pleaded in floods of tears with my doctor to find something to help me enjoy life. I was battling so bad with the thoughts that I should be shouting from the rooftops with happiness, having been given this glorious gift of life. However, I barely had the energy to pick up a ladder to get up there. "Why are you so tired" my family would say when my enthusiasm to get off the sofa was very minimal. I had to conserve all my energy for my work and everything else had to take a back seat. I began to get angry because no one seemed to understand the level of exhaustion I was feeling.

Last winter (2016) I visited the GP yet again as I had picked up the fifth chest infection in a row and was beginning to worry. He did the blood tests immediately and included a check on my Vitamin D levels. They came back dangerously low which gave the answer not only to the infections but to the increasing chronic fatigue I had experienced for three years. I now take 1000iu per day, doubled up in the winter months. So far this year I have only had 1 infection and boy have I got energy. I feel my energetic spirit for life has returned hallelujah! It is only recently I discovered that a study by Canadian researchers suggests that lower vitamin D levels during winter months may affect Tamoxifen's effectiveness. This would scarily increase the risk of cancer reoccurrence.

The researchers found that from January to March, the women had lower levels of vitamin D3, as well as lower levels of the active form of Tamoxifen compared to levels measured from July to September:

- Levels of the active form of Tamoxifen were about 20% lower than average in January to March
- Levels of the active form of Tamoxifen were 8% higher than average in July to September

This is the first study to suggest that low vitamin D levels may interfere with Tamoxifen's benefits.

Anti-sickness Tabs

There are different types of drugs used to control nausea and vomiting in cancer care.

Over the past 20 years, the drugs used for cancer sickness have improved.

There are many different types of anti-sickness medicines. Your doctor decides which drugs to give you based on whether your sickness is caused by your cancer or its treatment, and your past medical history. I was prescribed **Domperidone and Ondasetron. Neither worked for me which is why I was hospitalised.**

The following are common anti-nausea medications:

- Aprepitant (Emend®)
- Dolasetron (Anzemet®)
- Granisetron (Kytril®)
- Ondansetron (Zofran®)
- Palonosetron (Aloxi®)
- Proclorperazine (Compaz

Here are some tips to try which may help ease the sickness.

Fluids:

- Drink fluids throughout the day like water and juices. It is important to replace the fluids lost to avoid getting dehydrated.
- Avoid drinking liquids with meals.

Eating hints:

- Eat small amounts of food throughout the day.
- Eat before you get too hungry.
- Eat dry foods such as dry cereal, toast, or crackers without liquids especially first thing in the morning.
- Avoid heavy, high fat and greasy meals right before chemotherapy.
- Do not eat your favourite foods during this time. They will no longer be favourite foods if you begin to associate them with nausea and vomiting episodes.

Surroundings:

- Don't lay flat for at least two hours after eating. Rest by sitting up or reclining with your head elevated.
- Fresh air and loose clothing may be helpful after eating.
- Exercising after eating may slow down digestion and increase discomfort.

Turmeric tabs

I take one turmeric tablet a day (available from health stores). Turmeric is a spice that is often used as a food flavouring and has been used for many years in herbal remedies. There is currently no research evidence to show that turmeric can prevent or treat cancer but early trials have shown some promising results. The main active ingredient in turmeric is curcumin or diferuloyl methane, which laboratory studies have shown does have anticancer effects on cancer cells.

According to Cancer Research UK, A phase I clinical trial looked at giving curcumin to 25 patients with precancerous changes in different organs. This study seemed to show that curcumin could stop the precancerous changes becoming cancer.

Green tea

Not being keen on actual green tea, I take one green tea tablet a day also available from Health stores. It's clear that EGCG and other green tea antioxidants can stop cancer cells from growing, even directly kill them. They also seem to be able to prevent new blood vessels from forming within tumours that help cancer cells to grow rapidly and spread to other parts of the body. EGCG does this by interfering specifically with multiple biological mechanisms in cancer cells – and it appears to do so without affecting normal cells.

However, it must be remembered that so far the evidence for EGCG's anticancer abilities comes mainly from laboratory studies. Because of these promising results, many human clinical trials have been carried out (and are still being carried out) to find out whether EGCG and green tea extract supplements can indeed protect us from developing cancer.

While the results of these studies have not been as clear-cut as health experts would have liked, all the available evidence suggests that daily consumption of two to three cups of green tea can help to lower your overall cancer risk without any serious side effects

Floradix

Floradix contains organic iron (II) from ferrous gluconate, vitamins B2, B6, B12 and C which contribute to the reduction of tiredness and fatigue and to normal energy-yielding metabolism. In addition, iron contributes to normal red blood cell and haemoglobin formation which is supported by vitamins B6 and B12.

I keep a bottle of liquid Floradix in the fridge. Whenever I am feeling tired or less energetic, I literally take a swig from the bottle every morning for two or three days. It really does pick me up and give me the energy boost my body needs.

CHAPTER SEVENTEEN

Mission Self reset

The series of events I have just shared with you took away my spirit for a few years. Some close to me recognised this and some not. On reflection, the grief, sense of loss and recovery from my own illness had a massive impact on my ability to replicate the person I was prior to the breast cancer. The side effects from the medication, Tamoxifen, initially left me with chronic fatigue. This was harder to deal with than any of the treatment as at first it was not attributed to the medication. I had no idea why I felt so incredibly exhausted. My advice to anyone is to listen to your body and give it a break instead of like me, constantly fighting to live up to the expectations of others and constant demands of life. For five years I fought low moods and tiredness way beyond your wildest imagination. My alarm would sound in the morning and I would feel like id slept for five minutes. Someone most definitely had placed a led weight on my head because for the life in me I could not physically lift it from the pillow and that is no lie. My lack of energy would not allow me to be assertive in situations where it was essential, which resulted in detrimental circumstances that would add to my exhaustion. It was a vicious circle.

Once the five year remission passed it was like a light had switched on. My energy levels increased which was the catalyst for everything else to improve. I do think part of the reason for this is finally discovering the supreme combination of vital vitamins and essential foods that my mind and body has been craving. That actually sounds too easy. What I meant to say was because my energy levels increased it gave me the green light to make changes in my life that would enable me to start living, loving, embracing fun and family. It enabled me to start planning and setting goals. This was mission self-reset but my immediate thoughts were where do I start? I had to strip away and peel back the layers to look inside myself. I had been given the gift of life and it is this gift that is inspiring me to write. It is inspiring me to share with you some of the techniques I have put in place which will enable me to make changes. These changes are already empowering me to live and be happy in the moment. Let us be realistic here! This will not be without peaks and troughs. The techniques will intensify the peaks and reduce the troughs. They will provide you with the tools to work towards being the best person you can be. In a nutshell, that is my objective; to be the best version of ME. I will present the techniques in a series of short books so you can pick and choose the ones that will be most beneficial to you and your life. In short, my goal was and still is to restyle my mind and my physical self. That is easy isn't it? NOT! If it was so easy we would all be healthy, stick thin and achieving our desired goals without any effort. If it was easy I would have finished this book 3 years ago. Unfortunately it is painstakingly difficult even when you feel blessed to be who you are. For this reason the writing has and still is helping me to change. Believe me there are many adjustments that need to take place in my life but you have to start somewhere. Before you start, the first most important thing you need to know is WHY? Why do you want/need to make changes and what is your objective? Where to start is the biggest problem. So start with the end in mind. Begin by writing a list of what makes you happy and what makes you sad. Then look at the list and decide which take priority. Highlight those priorities. What I tend to do with work and personal projects, is put together a mini plan on excel. Create five columns with titles at the top. (Start with priorities) COLUMN 1– Why? What is it you want to achieve? COLUMN 2 – next step – what do you need to do next which will take you one step closer to your goal? / COLUMN 3 who will help you? – does anyone else need to help you achieve this step / COLUMN 4 by when? – Give yourself a deadline as to when you will execute this / COLUMN 5 date completed – put here the date you completed the task. Then underneath each priority continue to create new rows with the next steps until you have planned when you will finally reach your goal.

I intend to continue to work on areas of my life that need tweaking and believe me the list is long. I have just been promoted in my career so that is another mission completed. I have normal family issues just like anyone else who has kids (adult kids). I try to help them in their lives but you can only do so much for someone else. Ultimately they have to want to be helped and want to make changes themselves. What you CAN do is make changes in your own life. You cannot always influence what happens externally but you have choices in how you react and deal with situations.

Generally my eating habits are healthy however a few less pounds would not go a miss. Chocolate is my downfall. The Tamoxifen definitely contributed to the extra pounds (that is my excuse and I am sticking to it) – seriously when I began my medication, I literally blinked and I had put on half a stone. I never made massive changes to my diet because I refused to accept that my health had changed. Over the years I began to realise that what I eat has a massive effect on my energy levels consequently I have created some good habits and cleared some of the bad ones (a follow up book). Hopefully the following evidence will encourage you to make alterations to your eating habits. Please don't misinterpret my words here! We definitely don't need another diet but just need to make some healthy changes. Even if it is just one or two, it would be better than doing nothing. 20% of your efforts will equal 80% of your results so small changes will make a big difference. Prioritise your health by adopting a health first perspective. Start by choosing one healthy habit to stick to which will make everything else fall into place. For example, if your biggest obstacle to eating a healthy breakfast is that your time is limited, then prepare it the night before. Go to bed early, get up early and the rest will follow. Use the following evidence as your WHY?

On the 8th December 2017 there was a report in "The Telegraph" by Laura Donnelly, the Health Editor.

Research has found that:

- Losing weight can help women cut their breast cancer risk by up to a third.
- Experts said "modest" weight loss significantly cuts the chances of developing the disease.
- Six in ten British women are overweight or obese, with the highest rates of obesity among those in middle age.
- Excess weight raises the risk of breast cancer as fat cells produce hormones that help drive tumours.

But until now, it was not clear whether the risk could be reduced, by a successful diet. Around 50,000 women are diagnosed with breast cancer each year – with 12,000 dying.

- Four in five cases occur in women after they have gone through the menopause.
- The US research tracked more than 61,000 women aged between 50 and 79 for 11 years.
- It found those who lost five per cent of their weight saw their breast cancer risk fall by 12 per cent.
- And the risk fell by 37 per cent for postmenopausal women who slimmed down by 15 per cent.
- For a 12 stone woman who is five foot five inches tall, this would mean losing almost two stone.

Lead researcher Dr Rowan Chlebowski, from the Department of Medical Oncology and Therapeutics Research at City of Hope in Duarte, California, said: "Relatively modest weight loss was associated with significant lowering of breast cancer incidence. From this study, we have evidence that a weight loss strategy can be effective in lowering breast cancer risk in postmenopausal women."

The findings were presented at the San Antonio Breast Cancer Symposium.

Baroness Delyth Morgan, Chief Executive at Breast Cancer Now, said action on the findings could save lives. She said: "This important study provides further, clear evidence that postmenopausal women can significantly reduce their risk of breast cancer by taking steps to lose weight.

"Breast cancer risk increases with age. Being overweight after the menopause does increase your risk of the disease, likely because fat tissue becomes a women's main source of oestrogen after the menopause.

"The less body fat you have, the lower your oestrogen levels, which can decrease your breast cancer risk." Improved fitness and cutting down alcohol could also reduce the risk of breast cancer, she added.

Laura Donnelly, HEALTH EDITOR

This is an additional adjustment we can make that is not only going to have a positive effect on our general wellbeing and self-esteem but will assist in fighting off and standing up to cancer. It is something that we can influence and have control over.

I truly hope you follow and join me on my journey.

You can contact me by email - pinkhammerton@gmail.com

I would love to hear from you.

Thank you enormously from the bottom of my heart for allowing me to share my message with you.

All my love Jane (AmouraJ Kellett)☺

Printed in Great Britain
by Amazon

23947103R00067